Why The Purchase of *Breathing in Christ* Supports the Homeless Memorial Blanket

BREATHING IN CHRIST is a book about remembering who we are and Whose we are. It invites us to slow down, reconnect with the presence of Christ, and rediscover the dignity and life God breathes into each of us.

Yet, every year in communities across our country and around the globe, people die while experiencing homelessness. Often unnoticed. Often unnamed. Often without the dignity every human being deserves. The Homeless Memorial Blanket Initiative was created to remember and honor those lives.

Each blanket represents a person who has died while experiencing homelessness. Thousands of compassionate artisans stitch each one with love and care, creating a powerful reminder that every life matters and every person deserves to be remembered.

Each year, on the longest and darkest night of the year, these blankets are gathered from communities across the country and brought together in one powerful display of remembrance and love. Then, in a beautiful act of compassion and hope, the blankets are immediately distributed to individuals who are currently experiencing homelessness, offering warmth, dignity, and a tangible sign that they are seen, remembered, and not alone.

This book is about remembering the life and dignity Christ breathes into each of us. Supporting the Homeless Memorial Blanket Initiative is one small way of living that truth – remembering those the world often overlooks and honoring the sacred worth of every human life.

For this reason, 100% of the proceeds from this book support the Homeless Memorial Blanket Initiative.

Endorsements

I HAD THE PRIVILEGE of working with Marsha Roscoe for ten years in ministry. This work traces her spiritual journey in a demanding context and offers a guide for sustaining a healthy spiritual life amid the pace of modern life – a refreshing breath of Christ's spirit.

BISHOP JIM DUNLOP
Bishop (retired), Lower Susquehanna Synod, ELCA

READING THIS BOOK WAS inspiring, refreshing, soothing. Marsha helps us bridge the gap between what we know in our heads and what we trust in our hearts-the difference between belief and behavior. She shows us that God is as near as our next breath, offering hope, confidence and unconditional love.

Marsha offers a guide to move us from beleaguered to blessed, from exhausted to embraced, from weary to whole. Marsha invites us to see Jesus in our everyday moments meeting us where we are and calling us over the gap of exhaustion, fear and worry to a place of rest, release and wholeness.

This is an invitation to slow down. To breathe. To see ourselves as God sees us-beloved. And then, to adjust the rhythm of our lives for wholeness and peace. Breathe in. Breathe out. Breathe in Christ.

This is a great book that I will return to again.

THE RT. REV. AUDREY C. SCANLAN
Bishop, Episcopal Diocese of the Susquehanna

I HAVE RARELY READ a book so charmingly inviting, so gentle, so honest, about the hectic pace of life and how many of us need to move beyond stressful ways of being in the world. Marsha Roscoe is a gifted writer; vulnerable, tender (and funny.) She's been there. Her guidance is sensible and full of healing touches. It is spiritually-rooted but so very down to earth. Breathing in Christ is practical. It just may be life-changing as you learn faithful ways to dwell in Christ (even in your sleep!). You'll be glad in your identity as a beloved child of God.

Byron Borger,
Hearts & Minds Bookstore, Dallastown, PA

MARSHA'S BOOK AND HER spiritual wisdom is all about the rhythm God implants in our lives. She invites us to rediscover it, building from the most basic practice of attending to breathing and resting. She makes it a meditative journey of learning in our bones that in Christ we are fully loved. Go with her and find yourself taking gentle steps toward a renewed and more focused discipleship.

Gary Neal Hansen, Ph.D.
Author *Kneeling with Giants: Learning to Pray with History's Best Teachers*

Experiencing Jesus
In an Exhausting World

Marsha Roscoe

Charles Bruce Foundation
Carlisle, Pennsylvania

Title design - Heath Donnald

Copyright Charles Bruce Foundation & Marsha Roscoe ©2026

ISBN 979-8-9921607-4-1

FOR MY FATHER, whose journey with breath during lung cancer shaped these pages more than he could ever know and whose faith in me never ran out of air.

FOR JASON, who has been there from the beginning through every manuscript, loving, encouraging, and believing in me long before this book found its breath.

FOR GINA, who has grown up alongside this writing journey, nudging me to keep writing even in the darkness of winter and reminding me not to give up.

Table of Contents

Prologue

Introduction

Part 1: Discovering a Life of Breathing In Christ

Chapter 1: Tired of Being Tired 1

Chapter 2: Made From Rhythm, For Rhythm 7

Chapter 3: Our Divine Design 12

Interlude: A Simple Invitation from Creation to Nourish 35

Chapter 4: Vine & The Branches 41

Chapter 5: Living Sacred in the Everyday 48

Chapter 6: Holy Disruptions 56

Part 2: Becoming Whole

Chapter 7: Made From Love For Love 78

Chapter 8: Let It Be – Trusting God in the In-Between 83

Chapter 9: Naming Your Sources of Exhaustion 89

Chapter 10: Living From the Vine 125

Chapter 11: Rediscovering Values 129

Chapter 12: Setting Gentle Intentions: Planting the Seeds 139

Chapter 13: Discovering a Life of Breathing In Christ 148

Epilogue

Acknowledgements

Bibliography

PROLOGUE

You Don't Have to Hold Your Breath Anymore

BEFORE YOU DIVE into these pages, take a breath. Not just any breath: a holy one. The kind of breath that settles your body and reminds you: You are safe. The kind of breath that whispers to your soul: You are held. The kind of breath that helps your heart remember: You are not alone.

Let's begin here, because here's a truth worth holding close: you were never meant to live breathless. Not spiritually. Not emotionally. Not physically. Yet, so many of us do.

We hold our breath through the deadlines and the disappointments. We tighten our shoulders and clench our jaws, bracing ourselves against the weight of the day. We move through life wired, weary, and wondering why peace feels just out of reach. We wake up already feeling behind. Racing the clock. Running on caffeine and obligation. Filling every margin with noise. We tell ourselves we'll slow down soon. But soon keeps rescheduling. By the time we collapse into bed, we're exasperatingly depleted. The to-do list never finished. The slower pace we promised ourselves remains a far cry away.

In the middle of all the rushing and holding it together, a question rises. One we hesitate to speak out loud: Is this really the life Jesus intends for me?

This isn't the kind of tired a nap or weekend getaway can fix. It's a soul-level exhaustion. Your spirit has been carrying weight it was never meant to hold. Obligations pile up faster than rest can catch up. Expectations creep in. Joy takes a back seat. Peace barely gets a breath.

We keep showing up. We keep smiling. We keep going, always going, chasing the world's pace. Beneath the busyness, beneath the noise, underneath it all is a soul-level hunger for something more true. Gentler. Holier. A life that actually feels like living. A life rooted in Jesus. Peace that doesn't depend on fixing everything. Purpose that isn't tied to how much you get done. A relationship with Jesus where you are held (and discover you've been held the whole time).

From the very beginning, God's first gift was breath. "Then the Lord God formed humanity from the dust of the ground and breathed into their nostrils the breath of life…" (Genesis 2:7). You were breathed into being by a God whose love flows with every inhale. It was intentional. Intimate. Divine.

Even creation tells the story: Day turns into night. Work gives way to rest. Breath flows in and out. You were designed for this kind of rhythm. These are sacred patterns breathed into your body, your spirit, the shape of the life Jesus longs for you to live.

Every breath you take is more than just a biological function, it's a miracle wrapped in grace. The same God who bent low in the garden, who breathed life into dust and called it human, that same God is still breathing life into you. Right now. At this moment.

You don't have to hold your breath anymore. This book is an invitation to breathe again. Not just physically, though we'll pay attention to that too. Spiritually. Emotionally. Soulfully. To inhale grace and exhale all the pressure you've been carrying. To unlearn the patterns that have left you tired and disconnected. To realign your life with the rhythms God gives us. You will rediscover who you are, who you've always been, in Christ. Loved. Worthy. Whole. This book is an invitation to reclaim the sacred rhythm of living loved in Jesus.

We'll listen to our bodies. We'll examine the stories from which we've been living. We'll explore habits, beliefs, and holy rhythms that move us out of exhaustion. Through it all, we'll breathe. Because breath is both the path and the promise: a reminder that the Spirit of God is as close as your next inhale.

You don't have to hold your breath anymore. Let's begin again. Let's breathe in together. That restlessness you feel right now is sacred. It's the Holy Spirit's invitation. To find your way back to the rhythm God gave you. To breathe in the gift of life Jesus freely offers. To live in the love of Christ – who desires your heart, soul, and mind.

Introduction

The Life I was Missing

FOR A LONG TIME I lived wired and tired: always on, always needed, always a little behind.

From the outside, everything looked fine. More than fine, actually. I was productive. Reliable. The person you could count on. I met the deadlines. I answered the emails. I led the meetings. I showed up. I delivered. I gave my best to everyone else and that felt like faithfulness. Like I was doing what God called me to do.

On the inside, I was running on empty. My body was tired; my noisy mind was crowded with worry. My spirit was distant, disconnected, and void of joy. I had mistaken motion for meaning. I believed the faster I moved, the more I mattered. That if I could juggle it all without dropping anything, I was living out my calling. The emails didn't stop. The meetings kept stacking. There was always one more message to return, one more crisis to tend, one more deadline to meet. I was barely breathing.

It was a way of life that praised busyness and baptized it as success. A rhythm that celebrated hustle and called it holy, equating exhaustion with devotion. The fuller my calendar, the more "committed" I must be. The more tired I felt, the more faithful I was. I confused being needed with being known. I mistook productivity for purpose. I forgot that fruitfulness doesn't grow from burnout, it grows from abiding with Jesus.

What looked like success on the outside felt like a cage on the inside. Some might call it golden handcuffs. Everything looked right on paper. The salary was solid. The title carried weight. The calendar was full, the inbox never empty. To most people, it looked like I had made it.

The cost crept in so quietly, it was hard to notice at first. Harder to name. It wasn't the kind of cost you could see on a spreadsheet or list in a performance review. It was my health, in the way my body began to carry stress. It was my energy, drained before the day even started. It was the tension that found its way into my closest relationships, when I was too tired to be present, too distracted to listen, too depleted to love well.

Maybe the hardest part of all was how easy it was to miss. When you're constantly in motion, when you're checking all the boxes and showing up for everyone else, people rarely ask how you are. I had stopped asking myself, too.

The hardest part to admit is that underneath it all, the engine driving my life wasn't faith. It wasn't peace. It wasn't Jesus. It was fear. Fear of letting someone down. Fear of falling behind. Fear of not being good enough. Fear that if I stopped, even for a breath, I might feel all my feelings. Eventually, even the strongest engines burn out. What I needed wasn't more fuel for the hustle, it was a different way to live.

I didn't consciously choose a breathless life. It just – happened. Life picked up speed and I followed. I packed my calendar until there was no room left for resting or breathing. I said yes to every request, even when I should have said no – or at least not right now. When my body began to protest with headaches, digestion issues, and fatigue, I refused to listen. Isn't that what we're taught capable, faithful people do? You show up. You press on. You hold it all together, at all costs.

It worked. Until it didn't. There came a moment, slow and painful, when I could finally name what I had been avoiding: I wasn't truly living life. I was managing it. Coordinating it. Holding life together like a house of cards, praying the slightest breeze wouldn't knock everything down.

Here's the hardest part to confess: I still loved Jesus. I still prayed. I still led worship and wrote devotions. I still cared deeply for the people around me. I still showed up with a smile and gave my best. And I was So. Very. Very. Tired.

I knew how to talk about grace like a pro. I could quote scripture, teach it with conviction, and share it freely with others. Knowing God's promises isn't the same as living them.

I hadn't yet learned how to receive grace for myself. I didn't know how to let Jesus' love reshape the frantic pace I kept, soften the way I spoke to myself, or give me permission to slow down and simply breathe. It's one thing to believe in God's promises; it's another to live as if they're actually true.

What I really needed wasn't another time-saving hack or productivity tool. I didn't need one more thing to organize or perfect. I needed something deeper. I needed a whole new way to live. More than talking about Jesus, I wanted to experience Jesus, right in the middle of my everyday life.

Maybe you've felt this way, too. The exhaustion underscoring all the doing. The heaviness that settles in between the meetings, the care-giving, the endless expectations. Your soul is sighing for something more.

Maybe you know how to keep going. To perform. To meet the needs. To show up for others. Deep down, you wonder, What would it look like to live whole? Whole in Christ. Rooted. Fully alive.

Sometimes we can sense the growing gap between the life we're living and the life we were created for. A soul-deep longing for something truer, gentler, freer. Not just a better schedule. Not just another strategy. Permission to stop, breathe, and experience the life God is still offering.

That's what a life of Breathing in Christ is really about. It's waking up to the gentle, liberating truth that your soul was never designed to keep pace with the world's relentless demands. You were not created to run on empty, to hustle for worthiness, or to outrun exhaustion. You were created for something deeper. A way of living that flows from Christ's peace, not from cultural pressure. A rhythm that moves at the speed of grace, not urgency.

Breathing in Christ isn't one more thing to add to your already full list. It's an invitation to release what was never yours to carry and receive what has always been yours in Christ. It's about remembering what Jesus said so clearly: Jesus is the vine, we are the branches (John 15). Held. Nourished. Sustained.

Here's what I wish someone had told me much sooner and maybe what your heart needs to hear, too: You are not the problem. Your exhaustion isn't a weakness. It's not a failure of faith or discipline. You're tired because you've been running a race you were never meant to run. The world rewards overwork and calls it success.

Jesus offers another way, it's the way of truth and life. A holy rhythm that's already here, already moving through your breath, body, and spirit.

This book grew out of a simple but life-changing invitation from Jesus: stay connected to Me by inviting Me into every part of your day. The messy parts and the not-so-messy parts. The ordinary moments, the parts that don't go as planned. One breath at a time, right where you are.

This is your invitation to loosen the grip and discover that you don't have to hold it all together anymore. Instead, let yourself be held by Jesus and experience life in the One who sees you, loves you, and claims you.

This is a life of Breathing in Christ.

What This Book Is (and Isn't)

This is not a self-help manual. It's not a 10-step plan to optimize your mornings or a checklist to wring more productivity out of your already-overcrowded days. (If that's what you were hoping for, you may have wandered into the wrong aisle. I'm so glad you've found your way here anyway.) This is something different. This is not a book about striving harder. It's a book about breathing deeper, returning to the sacred rhythm you were made for and from. Learning how to live held more than hurried.

We live in a world that glorifies hustle, worships productivity, and hands out gold stars for burnout. Jesus invites us into a quieter, truer, more spacious way. What he calls the unforced rhythms of grace (Matthew 11:28-30, The Msg). The rhythm of breath and holy presence. The rhythm of being rooted, nourished, and sustained.

This book is my invitation to you to step off the treadmill of striving. To exhale the pressure to perform. To receive the life that's already being offered. Right here, right now, in the middle of your real, ordinary, beautiful, messy life. Not someday. Not when you finally catch up. Today. Day in and day out. Breath in and breath out. Discover a life of Breathing in Christ.

What You'll Find Inside

This book is about learning to live differently: gently, intentionally, rooted in grace. It's not about dramatic overhauls or chasing the next quick fix. It's about small, meaningful shifts that open space for the life God is already offering you. Inside these pages, you'll discover simple practices to help you reconnect: to your breath, to your body, to your rhythms, and to Christ's ongoing presence within and around you. Each step is an invitation to return to yourself, to peace, to God.

This book is for anyone who has ever said, "I want to slow down; I'm not sure where to begin." "I long to live with more purpose, and yet, I feel stuck." "I love Jesus – and I'm so very tired."

If any of that sounds familiar, welcome. You are not alone.

How This Book Moves
(Slowly, On Purpose)

The journey ahead is divided into two parts. This isn't a race or a checklist. The kind of change we're talking about here doesn't happen through willpower or quick fixes. It happens the way most good and holy things grow: slowly, intentionally, and with care. This book moves gently, like grace does, and it invites you to move that way, too. There's no need to rush. Go at the pace your soul needs. When something stirs your heart or resonates deeply, pause there. Linger. Breathe with it. Talk to Jesus about it. This is more than reading; it's a return to who you are in Christ. A return to the holy rhythm you were made for. A return to Holy breath, to Jesus' presence, to God's love.

Breathing Again

The first movement of this journey is about learning to breathe again; not just with your lungs, but with your soul. It's about remembering who you are at your core and how you were lovingly made. Before the hustle became your default. Before the noise drowned out your peace. Before exhaustion began to feel normal. This part of the journey invites you to gently return to your origin story, Creation, your sacred beginning. The place where God formed you from the dust and breathed life into your being. Before you did anything, achieved anything, or proved anything, God gave you breath. That was the beginning and it still is.

You were created with intention. Formed in rhythm. Rooted in love. This first section invites you to slow down enough to notice where you've been running on empty, and to reconnect with the steady, sustaining breath of God that's been with you all along.

This part of the journey is also about rediscovering your divine design, these beautifully sacred rhythms crafted into your body, mind, and spirit from the very beginning. You were created with an internal rhythm that mirrors the wisdom of creation itself. As we explore this, we'll consider the gift of circadian rhythms: how your body knows when to rest, when to rise, when to slow down, and when to seek light. Your body tells the truth, even when your schedule doesn't. We'll gently reflect on how disconnection from these God-given patterns often leads to the exhaustion we carry.

This is the work of noticing and remembering. Noticing where life has slipped out of rhythm. Remembering the grace that never left. Paying attention to breath and body, light and dark, waking and resting, the sacred cycles that promise this is the life you were made for.

Realigning with the rhythms that sustain life is how we begin to prepare the soil. This first movement of the journey is an invitation to slow down and listen. To connect what we so often keep separate: our spirituality, our biology, our patterns of living. We begin to participate again in the sacred rhythm God built into our being. From remembering to practicing. From breathless to breathing. From exhaustion to wholeness.

It's too easy for us to treat our spiritual life like a separate box. One we open on Sundays or in anxious moments, while our emotions, physical health, mental well-being, and everyday choices live in other boxes entirely. We've been conditioned to compartmentalize. As if following Jesus happens in one realm, while the rest of life moves (or spins) in another. That's not how you were created.

You are one whole, beautifully complex being, made in the image of God. Your soul and your body are not separate. Your mind is not disconnected from your spirit. Your breath, your biology, your emotions, your faith: it all belongs. And it all matters.

The rhythms God birthed into creation were designed for your whole being. Light and dark. Work and rest. Inhale and exhale. They are sacred rhythms meant to shape how you live, how you breathe, how you move through each day. Your body was designed to follow them. Your spirit was made to breathe in grace at their pace.

This book holds that truth at its core. It brings together the spiritual and the practical, theology and behavioral science, emotional well-being and habit formation, as partners in a whole and holy life as invitations. Yes, we'll talk about energy and time. About rest and rhythms. About your habits and your values. About your actual breath. Because these ordinary, everyday experiences are the sacred places where renewed energy begins. This is where your faith meets your breath; your choices meet your values; your beliefs about Jesus meet your habits, and your longing for peace meets the pace of your actual life. This is the journey of breathing again, stepping into a life of Breathing in Christ, to come home to the whole, integrated life God dreamed for you. To catch your breath again, one gentle inhale at a time.

Becoming Whole

The second part of this journey builds gently on the first. Once you've had space to breathe again, to notice, to realign, to prepare the soil of your life, we'll move a bit deeper into understanding who you truly are in Christ. This part of the journey is about identity. The habits we hold, the choices we make, the pace we keep, all of these are shaped by what we believe about ourselves and what we believe about Jesus. Here, we begin to ask: What stories am I telling myself about who I am? Are those stories aligned with the truth of my belovedness? What beliefs have been quietly fueling my exhaustion, my striving, my disconnection? Where am I living out of scarcity instead of grace? Out of fear instead of faith?

Part Two invites you to explore these deeper layers so that you come home to yourself. The self Jesus has loved all along. The self who is already worthy, already chosen, already held.

Together, we'll begin to look at how intentions, rooted in your identity, can become guiding principles in your life. We'll explore how small, intentional choices can align your daily rhythms with the peace and presence of Christ, as a way of living loved.

You may feel the need to stay with Part One for a long time. To linger in the breathing. The noticing. The remembering. That is holy work. There is no rush to move on. Part Two will be here when you're ready, waiting like an open door, not a deadline.

When the time comes, Part Two invites you to move beyond practicing habits into living a life of Breathing in Christ. This is the long, slow, beautiful work of becoming whole. One breath at a time.

How to Read This Book

These pages are meant to be savored. This isn't the kind of book you speed through; it's one you return to, pause with, and let unfold slowly as each section has time to breathe. I pray that it meets you where you are, and you give it time to land.

You'll find reflection prompts, breath prayers, and simple practices throughout these chapters as invitations to pause. To notice. To breathe. To encounter Christ in the middle of your actual, everyday life. There is no finish line here. No gold star for completing every prompt. This book is a companion, not a project – a gentle guide to help you remember what your soul may have forgotten. So, take a deep breath and allow Jesus' grace to lead. Let's begin Breathing in Christ, together. One breath, one moment, one holy step at a time.

PART ONE

Experiencing Jesus In An Exhausting World
Discovering A Life Of Breathing In Christ

Chapter One
Tired of Being Tired

"COME TO ME, all you who are weary and are carrying heavy burdens, and I will give you rest." - Matthew 11:28

Many of us are holding our lives together with a thread of faith – and maybe a double shot of espresso.

We love Jesus. We believe in God. We're trying – really trying – to do what's right. We pour ourselves into our families, our work, our communities, often without pausing to notice how little we have left for ourselves. Some days, everything gets done. The tasks are checked off. The people around us are fed, helped, encouraged. Still, after falling into bed with nothing left to give, we remain empty.

This is more than being tired. It's about where we are tired. We're carrying a kind of tiredness that sleep alone can't fix. We've got crowded schedules and constant noise, leaving us tired in the mind, tired in the body, tired in the heart and soul. We're chasing after a life we don't have time to live and we're too tired to figure out where to begin. We're so used to being tired we hardly notice it anymore. Exhaustion has become the norm and fatigue is our baseline. Burnout is practically a badge of honor. We've confused running on empty with faithfulness.

So, we cope. We smile. We reply to text messages while stopped at red lights. We answer emails between errands and scroll through news headlines while cooking dinner. We hold space for everyone else's needs and manage others' expectations like full-time crisis negotiators. Deep down, beneath the noise and rising above all the shoulds, we remember, this isn't the life Jesus promises us.

This world runs on tired, desperate to feel God's nearness, yet stuck in the speed of our own doing. We want to feel close to Jesus and can't seem to find a quiet moment to slow down. We pray for peace and we aren't sure how to let go. We keep moving because we don't know how to stop. We chase the next thing, the next task, the next role, the next *yes*, hoping it will finally be enough. We try to measure up to standards we didn't set and expectations we never agreed to. We don't even know who we're trying to convince anymore. All we know is this: it's exhausting.

The culture around us has trained us well in the art of exhaustion. According to the American Psychological Association, more than one in four Americans say they are so stressed they can't function. Seriously? One out of every four people. At the grocery store. In your pew. Sitting across from you on Zoom with the camera off. People keep showing up – smiling, serving, doing what's expected – while silently carrying a weight that feels heavier by the day. Maybe that's where you find yourself, too. Overwhelmed. Overextended. Over it.

The pandemic rewired our routines. Work came home and, in many ways, it never really left. The dining room table turned into an office. The kitchen became the breakroom. Our phones demand 24x7 attention with emails, group chats, and notifications. Now, too many of us are stuck in "always on" mode: Always connected. Always available. Always telling ourselves, "Just one more thing, then I'll rest."

The world isn't doing us any favors when it comes to slowing down. Case in point: I recently ordered new sheets – just sheets.

I was trying to make my bed feel more restful, more sacred. You know, like a grown-up human who values sleep. When they arrived, I noticed something odd: the sheets had pockets. Not for a book or a tissue or even ChapStick. No, these were phone pockets right by your head. Built-in bedtime phone holsters. Constant connection. Instant access.

It was funny – and not. It revealed something about the world we live in and what it assumes we can't live without. We've reached the point where even our bedding assumes we can't bear to be more than six inches away from a screen.

That little pocket stitched into my sheets reminded me how deeply embedded the noise has become and how desperately we need another way. A slower way. A way that doesn't require us to be "on" all the time. Mere survival was never meant to be the shape of our lives. Jesus never asked us to live at this pace. Jesus invites us to abide in Him. To live in rhythms that restore our bodies rather than deplete our souls. To experience an abiding connection with Jesus that heals our weariness rather than drains our energy.

That's what this journey is about. Unlearning what the world says we need. Relearning what Jesus already gives. Reclaiming the sacred rhythms of rest, breath, and grace. One small step at a time. One quiet pocket of peace at a time. One deep breath of Christ-centered life at a time.

Maybe the real question isn't just, Why am I so tired? Perhaps it's, What am I reaching for when I feel restless? or, Why does my phone feel like the thing I can't put down even when what I'm really longing for is peace? What we're really longing for isn't just entertainment or distraction, it's real connection. A place where our souls can exhale and feel at home.

Our beautifully made, God-designed bodies are trying to get our attention: sleepless nights, shallow breathing, racing thoughts, that persistent pain in your shoulders or the tightness in your chest. We chalk it up to stress, to busyness, to being human. These aren't just quirks or bad days. They're signals, gentle alerts from your body and spirit, reminding you that you've drifted from the sacred rhythms your soul was created to follow.

I've lived this story, too. I know what it's like to build a life that looks together from the outside while empty on the inside. I know what it's like to let the buzz of my phone drown out the still, small voice of God or to give more attention to the next task than to the breath God placed in my lungs. Here's what I've also come to believe deeply, personally, and wholeheartedly: Life doesn't have to be this way. Into all this exhaustion, effort, and noise, Jesus speaks, "Come to me, all you who are weary and are carrying heavy burdens, and I will give you rest." (Matthew 11:28)

Jesus welcomes you in the now, not in the someday. Bring the weight of what you've been carrying. Bring the noise, the needs, the numbness. Come when your heart is heavy and your mind is racing. Come with your half-formed prayers and unfinished lists. Come carrying whatever you're holding. Come, and I will give you rest.

This is more than sleep. More than time off. More than stepping away from responsibility. It's a soul-deep rest that restores your humanity, revives your spirit, and reminds you of your true identity. It's rest that reminds you of your sacred worth. You are more than what you do. Rest offers a way of moving that makes room for breath. This kind of rest renews your sense of self and reconnects you to Who and what truly matters. It reminds you that your value is not earned, it's already given through love. Jesus offers more than strategies or steps, Jesus offers Himself with life that breathes, a life shaped by love and a life that remembers who you truly are – beloved, whole, enough.

This isn't just about catching your breath after another long, demanding day. Jesus invites you into a whole new way of being, one that doesn't wait for vacation or burnout to give you permission to rest. This is a rhythm shaped by grace that steps off the treadmill of performance and into the wide, open space of peace. It's a life where rest is the rhythm – not the reward and a life where your worth isn't measured by how much you get done – but receives its value in Jesus. Your soul gets to breathe in the middle of the ordinary, and small moments become holy ground.

If you're weary, it may be your soul's gentle way of inviting you home, returning to what has always been true: You were made for rest. You were made for communion with the One who knows you by name, and for a way of living that feels more like grace than pressure. This kind of rest is available right here, in the middle of your real, messy, beautiful life. It begins with turning toward Jesus, just as you are. Come as you are.

Take a deep breath as Jesus meets you there and lifts what's been too heavy for too long.

When I Couldn't Breathe

In the spring of 2014, my father's cancer diagnosis came like a jolt to the heart. The prognosis, we were told, was hopeful. The doctors spoke with optimism, and we clung on to that hope like a lifeline (as I did my own late-night *Google MD* research). We prayed with faith while we hoped with caution.

Then, without warning, the complications came fast and without mercy. Just the day before, my father had undergone surgery to remove a few small nodules from his lung. The procedure was meant to be routine. Soon after surgery, something just was not right. His breathing changed, shallower, slower. His face began to look subtly swollen, almost like he was holding his breath beneath the skin. Then the truth became undeniable, something was very wrong.

During surgery, nodules had been removed from the lower cavities of his lung, leaving small openings where the tissue had been cut away. They inserted biological plugs to seal the holes, something routine and usually effective. In my father's case, one of the plugs never anatomically adhered to his lung, causing a slow air leak inside his chest cavity, with no path to escape. With each breath, air slipped through the unsealed hole into his chest.

When air escaped from the lung and entered the chest cavity – a space that should have remained sealed – it began to build pressure around the lung instead of inside it. The trapped air pushed against the lung tissue, preventing it from fully expanding. Medically, it's called a pneumothorax.

As pressure increases, the lung begins to collapse, and the heart and other organs can be compressed as well. In essence, it's the body's way of fighting to breathe, which can cause breathing to become strained and shallow.

What happened on the inside started to show up on the outside. His face swelled, especially around his eyes and cheeks. When you touched his skin around the neck and chest, you could hear it crackle due to the air bubbles lodging underneath his skin, which stretched so tight it looked painful. His face was changing, tight and swollen. It became harder and harder to recognize him as his eyes disappeared under the swollen flesh. The man lying in that hospital bed didn't look like my dad anymore. He looked like someone being suffocated from the inside out.

There I was, sitting at the edge of his bed, frozen in place. I could feel my own body reacting, my chest tightening, my throat closing in, my breath growing short. I wanted so badly to help him, to ease the pain, to swap places, to make it all go away. Yet, all I could do was sit there, heart breaking and lungs aching as I watched his discomfort expand. At that moment, I couldn't breathe either.

Then, something caught my eye, the edge of my journal sticking out from behind a folded blanket on the windowsill. Almost instinctively, I reached for it and flipped it open, the pages falling to a recent entry I barely remembered writing just a few days earlier. One line nearly jumped off the paper, "Breathing in Christ requires trust."

I stopped cold because the words hit like a deep inhale after being underwater too long. I could almost hear the Spirit say, "This isn't yours to carry. You can't fix it. You can't force breath into his lungs. You can, however, trust Me with what you can't control."

It was as if God gently placed an oxygen mask over my soul, not to take away the pain, but to help me breathe inside it. I became aware – deeply aware – that I wasn't alone. Jesus was there in the sacred stillness of that hospital room, and I knew that God was holding us both in the same holy breath. The same Spirit that hovered over creation was hovering here now, breathing life even in the midst of deep fear.

Finally, my body remembered what it meant to breathe. I breathed out and let go. Let go of the illusion that I could control what was happening. Let go of trying to spiritually micromanage my father's suffering. I let God be God and let grace hold the space I couldn't fill. I was able to sit with my father in silence, without trying to fix or to solve, just to be together. I could stay present in the discomfort, even without answers, because I knew we weren't alone. Jesus was there, breathing with us.

There was, by God's grace, an unexpected path forward.

By grace, later that day we were presented with another option, a newer approach that gently rotated his body from side to side in a specialized hospital bed. The rhythm was meant to encourage his lung to seal, to help the air escape, and to give him space to breathe again. We were not guaranteed healing. By God's grace, his body responded. The trapped air cleared, his swelling decreased and normal breathing returned to his body: and so did time. He lived for eleven more years.

Eleven more years of breath, giving us time we never thought we'd have. Time to laugh again, to heal the past, to gather around dinner tables and enjoy his favorite cherry crumb pies and time to simply be together in ways we didn't take for granted anymore.

Perhaps you know what it's like to live in that space: waiting, holding, bracing. Maybe your version of the hospital room looks like the office, the kitchen, the sanctuary pew. Maybe you're there now; holding your breath through meetings and meals, trying to hold up your family, your work, your world. Afraid that if you stop, even for a moment, the pain beneath the surface might finally catch up with you.

If that's where you are, let this be a holy interruption. You were never asked to carry all of this alone. The invitation of Jesus has always been this: There is another rhythm available to you. A rhythm that begins with, *Come to Me, all who are weary.* Come with your questions and your overwhelm. It's the rhythm of Jesus, already moving beneath the surface of your life.

A life of Breathing in Christ is not about starting over; it's about starting right where you are with your current life, your current pace, and your current breath, and letting grace meet you there. You were created to live in rhythm with Jesus. This journey is about small realignments rather than perfect routines or spiritual performance. Holy pauses. Honest noticing.

Beyond the fatigue and busyness, your soul trusts that something more is possible. You were made to walk at the pace of love as you move in rhythm with Jesus. It begins with the courage to notice: to notice your tiredness, your body's tension, the heaviness in your chest or the pain you've been pushing past for too long. It begins when you recognize, maybe for the first time or the hundredth, I can't live like this anymore. Hear this: you don't have to live like this anymore. Jesus is simply inviting you to come, tired as you are, burdened as you are, to experience all He has to offer.

This, right here, is a turning point. In these moments of awareness and honesty, grace meets you. From here, something new can begin, a holy unlearning as you discover a life that breathes in Jesus.

Chapter Two
Made From Rhythm, For Rhythm

IN THE VERY first pages of Scripture, we're invited into a sacred beginning as we witness the sacred choreography of God's creativity. Our creation stories are a testament to the gentle, rhythmic unfolding of life itself. God shapes the world with intention, with breath, with pauses built in – not as an afterthought – as a holy part of the divine design.

The story of Creation tells us more than what God made. It invites us to pay attention to how God made it. It reveals a truth we often forget in our fast-paced lives: God created with rhythm. Not chaos. Not urgency. Not the pressure to get it all done in a day. With intention. With breath. With rhythm.

Genesis moves like a holy choreography – a slow dance – where every element has its moment. First light, then dark. First evening, then morning. First work, then rest. Step by step, breath by breath, God speaks life into being with beauty, balance, and care.

The heart of Genesis is showing us that the way we live matters to God. Genesis 1 and 2 hold within them the DNA of our design: breath and pause, light and dark, effort and ease. They're holy patterns telling us what happened and they're showing us how to live. God's care extends beyond our survival into our flourishing. Our daily rhythms – how we breathe, how we rest, how we dwell fully in our bodies and our time – are part of what makes life holy.

Digging deeper into Creation, you will find two formational rhythms: time and place. Time teaches us to honor the natural flow of our days, to welcome the light and release the dark, to recognize when to begin and when to pause. Place reminds us that where we are matters just as much as what we do. Our souls find rest (not in constant movement) in being grounded in love, in belonging, in the presence of God.

Together, these rhythms shape how we live and how we experience life. They remind us that we were never meant to rush through our days or escape our present. We were made to be here. Now. In this time. In this place.

Genesis 1
Holy Time

And God said…and it was so…and there was evening, and there was morning, the first day (repeated throughout Genesis 1).

Genesis 1 shows how God moves, with a holy rhythm flowing through every word. God speaks, and creation listens. Light appears, the waters part, and life grows. Then, there's always a pause, a moment of stillness before the next breath of creativity. There was evening, and there was morning: the first day. The second. The third. Each one marked by the rhythm in which it was created. Each day follows a pattern, a rhythm, a sequence: a breath between each step. Creation itself is dancing and God is the choreographer.

It's easy to skim over the opening lines of Scripture. God made the world. Got it. Move on. These words are more than the beginning – they are a sacred rhythm meant to shape how we move through life. God, who held the power to make it all at once, chose instead to create in steps, in days, in divine pauses. Not for God's sake, but for ours. God knew we'd need the reminder: slow is holy.

Genesis 1 offers a holy question. Are we living in step with the rhythm God built into creation? The rhythm of light and dark, day and night, work and rest. Or, have we drifted into another kind of rhythm entirely? One shaped by glowing screens, endless scrolls, and midnight emails. Are we burning the candle at both ends, convincing ourselves we're just catching up; when – in truth – our bodies are longing for a sacred pause? The rhythm of God was never meant to exhaust us. It was meant to hold us.

Genesis offers a counter-narrative to the world that names hustle as heroic. It reminds us of a sacred pace, rhythm driven by grace before urgency. A rhythm where enough is truly enough. We were made to live in step with the God who breathed life into dust; to live with joy and to rest with trust. You were made to breathe. To rise with the light and rest with the dark. To wonder at the world instead of trying to conquer it. Your body, fearfully and wonderfully made, already remembers what your soul might have forgotten: the rhythm of Creation still pulses beneath everything and that rhythm is still yours to experience.

Genesis 2
Holy Place

Genesis 1 gives us a wide-angle view of creation's majesty: sun, moon, stars, oceans, and time itself unfolding in divine rhythm. Genesis 2 zooms in a bit tighter, moving from the vastness of the cosmos to focus on the intimacy of a single breath. Then the Lord God formed man from the dust of the ground and breathed into his nostrils the breath of life, and the man became a living being. And the Lord God planted a garden in Eden, in the east, and there God put the man whom God had formed. (Genesis 2:7-8)

From galaxies to garden soil, from God speaking life into existence to God kneeling low, forming humanity from dust, this is where intimacy takes place and love begins taking shape. It's a God who gets close enough to breathe into us, face to face. In a garden, a space intentionally planted by God, a space of peace, rhythm, and rest. A place to be held and nourished. A place to walk with God.

Notice where God places the very first humans. Not in a cathedral filled with rituals, not in a castle surrounded by luxury, and not at the summit of a mountain built by achievement or ambition. God places them in a garden, a living space cultivated with loving intention and care. A place of color and scent and soil; a place of flowers and fruit, of earth and air. A place to walk with God in the middle of the day. A place to belong. To delight. A place filled with life. Place has always mattered to God.

In the Creation story, God doesn't stop at forming the first human, God goes on to prepare a place. Eden becomes the context where relationships unfold, where God and humanity can walk together. Where we are matters just as much as who we are. The places we occupy – our homes, our workplaces, our communities – are not incidental. They are invitations. Invitations to notice God's presence and dwell with intention. From the very first breath, we are beings rooted in space and time.

Genesis 2 invites us to slow down and ask some honest questions. Am I creating space for God in my everyday life? Do the places I spend time help me notice Jesus' love, or do they make me feel rushed and distracted? Are the spaces I live in…my home, my heart, my habits, helping me grow in grace? Do they help me breathe easier, love deeper, and see Jesus more clearly? While we may not always get to choose where we are, we can choose how we are in those places. We can gently care for the parts of our lives that feel messy, busy, or forgotten. We can plant little habits of peace right where we are. At the kitchen table. In traffic. During a walk. At bedtime. The opening chapters of Genesis lay out a holy rhythm, a pattern of life rooted in purpose, rest, and relationship.

Genesis 1 teaches us to honor time by moving with the rhythm God built into each day. Genesis 2 reminds us your place matters, God meets you in the ground beneath your feet. Together, these opening chapters of Scripture form a sacred invitation: Live your days within God's rhythm. Move with Jesus in the garden of your real, everyday life.

The same breath that filled Adam's lungs still moves through you today. God's holy breath doesn't wait for perfect conditions and it's not reserved for holy places or set-apart moments. It's already here whispering into the deepest parts of your heart. This place matters. This moment is holy. You are not alone.

Disconnected from Rhythm

There was a season of my life I still find hard to talk about. Even now, when I think back, I feel a mix of disbelief and tenderness for the version of me who tried so hard to outrun her limits. I honestly believed that if I just worked harder, showed up to everything, and kept producing, then maybe, just maybe, I would feel like I was enough. The more I filled my calendar, the more faithful I thought I was. The busier I stayed, the more important I felt. Productivity became proof of purpose and efficiency became my virtue. At the time, it all seemed so noble, responsible. Even spiritual.

In hindsight, I was living on the edge of absurdity and managing chaos. My days were crammed with obligations, one stacked on top of the next like an unstable game of Jenga. Meetings back-to-back. To-do lists that grew faster than I could complete them. Every bit of margin erased. Every *yes* offered from a place of fear, not freedom. I wish I could tell you I went on retreat and came back after an epiphany to sort it all out. The truth is harder – and more human – to admit. I almost didn't include this part. It's tender. Embarrassing, even. If I'm being honest, and if we're walking in truth together, I need to say it. In the middle of my busyness, I started doing something I never imagined I would: I began double-booking people. On purpose. (Yes. You read that right.)

I told myself it was a clever fix. Too many people were canceling or rescheduling at the last minute. So, I thought, Why not schedule two at once? One will probably back out. Problem solved. What could go wrong? (You already know where this is going.)

Eventually, both people showed up. Same time. Same place. No buffer. No excuse. No hiding. Just me, face to face with the consequences of trying to outsmart and control my time and getting caught in the mess of my own bad math and, if I'm honest, poor theology.

Hindsight is always 20/20, isn't it? Looking back, I can see it clearly now. The real problem wasn't my schedule. It was how I had stopped seeing time as something that belongs to God. I started treating people like puzzle pieces. Something to squeeze into the small cracks of my day and still call it pastoral care. I was managing minutes, not nurturing relationships. I was checking boxes, not creating space for Jesus to show up. In trying to control everything, I lost sight of who and what mattered most.

I realized that the questions I had been asking weren't the ones my soul, or Jesus, needed. I stopped asking How can I fit more in? and began asking Does my schedule reflect the life that's possible in Jesus? Does my pace honor the person Christ invites me to become? Is there room here for what I truly value or am I just filling time and calling it faithfulness?

Our world loves to hurry. We live in a world glorifying packed calendars and speedy replies. Where busy and hurry are mistaken for success. Yet, Jesus never rushed. He walked. He paused. He listened. He noticed. He prayed. He spent time with God. He made time feel sacred. Jesus certainly never double-booked people. Jesus lived his values.

We weren't created to rush through life chasing checklists, running on coffee and sheer willpower. That kind of pace might impress the world, but it slowly drains the soul. We were made for a different kind of rhythm. A holy rhythm. One that breathes deeply. One that listens with love. One that slows down enough to see Jesus in the small, ordinary moments.

If you're tired today – really tired. If your neck is tight, your mind feels cluttered, and your body is begging for a break. If you've been living like your value depends on what you do, how much you manage, or how well you hold everything together. Then hear this with your whole heart: You are invited to return. To come back to the rhythm you were made from and for. Sometimes the holiest thing you can do isn't to put in more effort. It's simply making space. Space for grace. Space for Jesus. Space to breathe in Christ.

Chapter 3
Our Divine Design

EVEN RIGHT NOW, your body is living a symphony of sacred rhythm. As you read these words, your body is keeping time. Your breath rises and falls, almost unnoticed. Your heart beats beneath your ribs, keeping a rhythm you didn't have to create. Blink by blink, your eyes refresh. With every stretch, every sigh, every mid-afternoon yawn, your body speaks this truth: You were designed for rhythm. There are cycles at work within you every day. Even your hunger. Even your yawns. Even those midday dips in energy. All of these are holy signals, nudges from your body, reminding you of the pace you were made for. Here's the best news of all. This holy rhythm doesn't depend on you getting it right.

Your breath rises and falls nearly 20,000 times a day without effort, without your to-do list's permission. Twenty thousand quiet reminders, you are alive by grace alone. Your heart knows this rhythm, too, beating steadily, minute after minute. It speeds up when life feels intense. It slows down when you finally exhale and let yourself rest. Your blood travels more than 60,000 miles of vessels, enough to circle the globe twice, right there inside of you. A little miracle on repeat, whether you realize it or not.

Your digestive system knows the rhythm of restoration, breaking down food, absorbing nutrients, restoring energy without needing applause or permission. If today's meal choice is one you're rethinking – let grace do the heavy lifting there, too.

Even your brain joins the choreography within you, pulsing with waves helping you think clearly and sleep deeply. Your hormones follow their own holy cadence. Melatonin guides you into stillness while cortisol invites you into motion. None of it is accidental. Every rhythm reflects the loving design of a God who wired you for wholeness. This divine choreography continues to unfold, one breath at a time.

At the center of all these patterns lies your circadian rhythm, your inner timekeeper. This God-given cycle, roughly 24 hours long, comes from the Latin phrase circa diem, meaning "around a day." This sacred rhythm is designed to keep you connected to light, to earth, to your own body – to the holy dance of being fully human. You were designed to wake with the light and to slow down with the dark. Even when the world around us doesn't honor it, circadian rhythms naturally pulse within us, waiting to be noticed.

When morning light spills through your window, it's a divine invitation to Wake up. Begin again. Step gently into this new day of grace. When evening settles in and the light fades, your body responds, melatonin increases as your temperature begins to drop. Your breath slows down, and the invitation becomes clear. Rest now. Release the day. Let yourself be held. The rhythm you carry was intentional, breathed into your cells by a Creator who knew you would need them, filled with cues embedded all around you.

It's no wonder we forget. The world makes it easy. We override the signals and caffeinate instead of rest. We scroll past the sacred, eat on the run, and call five hours of sleep "good enough." The truth is, even in all the noise and neglect, the rhythm remains and it doesn't scold or shame. It simply waits for you to come home. Let's take a closer look.

Our Divine Design
6:00 p.m. - 10 p.m. Grounding

Evenings are for relaxing and connecting instead of heavy dinners - the grounding part of our day where we want to nourish and flourish. Think *water*!

10:00 p.m. - 2:00 a.m. Rest & Digest

If our stomachs are relatively empty, between 10:00 p.m. - 2:00 a.m. is a natural cleansing time for our bodies.

2:00 a.m. - 6:00 a.m. Restoring

This is when you are in the deepest part of your sleep, which is incredibly important for mental recovery. During these hours, our body is working hard to make that happen.

6:00 a.m. - 10:00 a.m. Wakefulness

As you wake up, a subtle transformation takes place as you transition from rest to activity. This energizes the body, readying us for the day ahead.

2:00 p.m. - 6:00 p.m. Focus

The brain requires an enormous amount of fuel to survive and work well. This is the time of day our brains need the most fresh air, sunlight and whole foods.

Or if you prefer to run morning to night - think of it this way:

Morning Rhythm 6:00 a.m. - 10:00 a.m.
A Sacred Beginning (Even If You Hit Snooze Three Times)

Mornings are both a beginning and a threshold, a doorway between the stillness of night and the unfolding of a brand-new day. Even before your eyes open, your body is already at work, preparing you for what's ahead. As the sun rises, your body follows suit, releasing cortisol, your natural, God-designed wake-up nudge. Think of it as an internal sunrise saying Wake up.

Of course, not every morning feels sacred. They feel more like, Where's the coffee and why are the pets already awake? The dog's pacing, the cat knocked something over. The coffee isn't brewing fast enough, and your phone is already pulling you in a dozen directions. Before we take our first deep breath, there are texts, news alerts, notifications, a to-do list that somehow grew overnight. Instead of noticing Jesus, we scramble into a day full of noise and urgency, and the weight of all we didn't finish yesterday. I know that rhythm. I've lived in it.

For a long time, I reacted before I got out of bed. The alarm blaring (honestly, who designed these terrible sounds?) and eyes barely focusing, I'd grab my phone almost instinctively running on autopilot. First, a few rounds of Words with Friends. Next, a scroll through headlines, social media, and everyone else's carefully edited lives. Before I even knew what I was thinking or feeling, I had already taken in a flood of voices, images, opinions, and comparisons. Have you noticed how, according to social media, by 5:30 a.m., it seems like everyone else is thriving and living their best life? Glowing. Sipping green juice. Crushing their goals. As for me, I hadn't even brushed my teeth.

Without even getting out of bed, I was already comparing my life to someone else's highlight reel, chasing their joy with a quick swipe and the occasional purchase I definitely didn't need. Take, for example, the morning Instagram convinced me that clearly what I needed was a sleek, top-of-the-line espresso machine. Yes, I bought it. Before 6:00 a.m. Half-asleep. From bed. I was convinced that this sleek, chrome machine complete with its built-in steamer wand and perfectly lit buttons was going to change my mornings. This was it, the thing that would usher in a whole new version of me: peaceful and caffeinated just right. Spoiler alert: the machine worked beautifully and no amount of espresso could calm a soul already running at full speed before sunrise. The peace I longed for wasn't found in the perfect cup of java. If caffeine alone could fix me, I'd be a walking miracle by now.

What I've come to realize is that my morning habits were more than filling time, they were forming me. Each day, the way I began the day was shaping the kind of person I was becoming. When I reached for my phone first, before my breath had even settled or my feet touched the floor, I was choosing noise over stillness. Scrolling through headlines, updates, and highlight reels became my default ritual. Without meaning to, I was training my heart for reactivity instead of receptivity. I was wiring my mind to compare before I had even grounded myself in God's truth and to rush into the day instead of receiving it as a gift. Mornings don't have to be a frantic race to catch up with the world.

There is another way to begin the day – a more spacious, sacred way that welcomes you gently into the gift of being alive. The first moments of the day carry more power than we realize. Before the noise of the world floods in, there's a sacred window of time when our hearts and minds are most impressionable. Like soil just turned, the morning is soft, open, ready to receive whatever we plant. And what we plant matters. Those first few moments shape the tone of the entire day. They frame how we see ourselves, how we see God, how we see what's possible. If we begin the day in reaction mode, we set a path of comparison and scarcity. If we embrace the morning hours for what they are intended to be, a gentle ease into the day, we often experience fewer challenges enjoying some quiet time for prayer or intention setting. We remind ourselves who we are and Whose we are before anything else can define us.

I've learned, sometimes the hard way, that when we begin to reclaim our mornings, we begin to reclaim our lives. These days, I begin differently. Not always perfectly, but with more intention, more awareness, and more kindness toward my own soul. I no longer wake up and immediately dive into the noise. Instead, I reach for breath before I reach for my phone. Before I let the voices of the world shape my heart, I pause and let my own breath remind me: I'm here. God is here. That is enough. I call it, "sky before scroll."

Instead of letting my screen be the first light I see, I let the morning sky greet me. I open a window or go outside to notice the color of the clouds or the sky and feel the air. I allow the light to touch my face. It doesn't take long and it makes a huge difference. I'm learning to let God have the first word.

What about you? How do your mornings meet you? We all have morning routines. Some we've chosen on purpose, others we've fallen into without even realizing. What's the first thing your eyes land on? The first thing your hands reach for? The first thought that spins through your mind before your feet even touch the floor? It's worth asking, gently, without judgment, Is this how I want to begin my day? Is this how I want to meet my life? What habit, what reflex, what pattern might be stealing my peace before I've even had the chance to take one full breath? Maybe you sleep a little longer than you planned. Not because you're lazy, but because your body is carrying the weight of yesterday's hurry and you woke up already tired, already feeling behind. Maybe you grab a quick bite on the way out the door, something fast, something sweet, hoping that a hit of caffeine or sugar will fill in for the rest you never fully received. You're moving, but hardly nourished. Maybe your morning moves in a straight line from bed to desk, from horizontal to hunched, without a single pause. No stretching. No breathing. No notice of the morning light.

It's so easy to miss the very things your body and soul are craving. It doesn't always feel catastrophic, at least not at first. Most of the time it just feels like another ordinary morning. Over time, those small decisions become patterns and those patterns begin to shape us. Sleeping past your natural rhythm might feel like a gift in the moment, yet it can throw off your internal clock, leaving you groggy instead of restored. That quick, heavy breakfast you grabbed on the go might satisfy your hunger for a moment, but it can slow digestion and drain your energy instead of fueling it. Skipping even a few minutes of gentle movement in the morning means your lymphatic system misses its wake-up call, losing the chance to clear out what your body needs to release and activate the natural energy meant to carry you into the day. If you miss the morning light altogether, your brain may still think it's time to sleep. Without that signal, melatonin lingers longer than it should, leaving you foggy and unfocused, even if you've technically had enough sleep.

These may seem like small things. Small things, repeated often enough, become the rhythm we live by. Slowly, almost imperceptibly, those rhythms can begin to pull us out of sync with our very design, rhythms rooted in light, breath, movement, and grace.

Breath Practice Before Your Day Begins

We miss it more often than we realize, rushing past our breath in the name of getting things done. When life feels too heavy, we don't even realize we're holding our breath, bracing life instead of breathing through it. Breath becomes background noise, almost an afterthought, instead of the anchor it was always meant to be. Breathing is an ever-present reminder that God is near, that we are still here, that life continues even when we're overwhelmed. Returning to breath is how we return to ourselves. And to God.

Before you move, before you scroll, before you reach for the to-do list or pour the coffee (even the espresso from that very persuasive Instagram machine), pause. The very first gift God gave humanity in the garden was breath. Just breath. A gift. A sign of life and a direct connection to the Spirit of God. Here's one small way to begin:

Sit at the edge of your bed, close your eyes if that feels right, allowing your hands to rest gently in your lap. Take three slow, steady breaths. As you breathe in, pray: Jesus, fill me. As you breathe out, release: I live in You.

That's it. Three breaths, one prayer, and Jesus meets you in the first few moments of your day.

Light: Step Into the Son. I mean Sun

There's a reason some of the very first words God speaks in Scripture are, "Let there be light." Not, "Let there be hustle." Not, "Let there be Wi-Fi." Light. Light, before anything else. Before time. Before form. Before breath. God called forth light. Light marks the start of something beautiful and alive; it can do the same for you.

Your body is designed to rise with the sun. Within about thirty minutes of waking, your internal clock (if you remember, this is what science calls your circadian rhythm) is quietly scanning your environment for cues. It's asking: Are we on? Are we awake? What's the vibe here? Here's the wild part, God already built the answer into the light. Natural sunlight doesn't just help you find your slippers or keep you from stepping on the dog's favorite squeaky toy, though that's a definite perk. Light literally sends a message to your brain and body: It's time to rise. It tells every system in your body, Let's begin. God, in divine brilliance, set this rhythm into your biology.

Open the curtains or door and let the light in, even if you're still wrapped in that 15-year-old robe you keep meaning to replace. Or, sit by a window with your coffee or tea. Or, walk the dog, feel the pavement under your feet, or simply stand on your porch for a moment, letting the light, however gentle or gray, greet your face. It doesn't have to be a clear blue sky. Even on overcast mornings, outdoor light is 10 to 100 times stronger than what your indoor lamps or screens can offer.

Starting your day with natural light improves your hormones and lifts your mood by clearing the mental fog that scrolling a newsfeed can't touch. It also does something holier. Light widens our view. It reminds us that we are not the center of the universe. We belong to something, Someone, much bigger than ourselves. The sky holds space we don't have to fill. The clouds keep moving whether or not your inbox is empty. The sun rises whether or not your to-do list is complete. The sky is still there, holding you. Kind of like Jesus.

Try pairing this moment of light with a breath prayer or simple gratitude. On your inhale, pray, "Light of the world…" On the exhale, "Shine in me." A few minutes outside, a glance at the sky, a pause while the coffee brews, is all it takes to notice what God gives you. You don't need the perfect sunrise or the ideal morning soundtrack; just notice Who is already there. Even if your weather app says "overcast," Jesus shows up. Every. Single. Time. God has already gone ahead of you, and the light is already here.

Water: Hydrate Before You Caffeinate

Before you reach for that cozy cup of caffeine, consider this: Your body has just spent the last 7 to 8 hours doing deep, sacred work. While you slept, doing absolutely nothing productive by the world's standards, your body was faithfully tending to what keeps you alive. It was repairing cells and healing small things you never even knew were broken. It was balancing your hormones, restoring your immune system, and clearing out yesterday's stress to make room for peace today. It was filing memories and resetting energy levels. All while you rested. All while you let go. This is the miracle of being human. You don't have to do anything for your body to carry out the sacred work of restoration.

All of that sacred work takes water. Your body wakes up dehydrated from all that overnight labor. Every exhale, every hour tucked under the covers, your body has been steadily becoming dehydrated. (It's not you, it's science). And what do most of us reach for first thing in the morning? The coffee pot. The Keurig. The espresso machine. (No judgment, you know my love affair with coffee). Your body could use a little bit of help getting ready for the new day. A simple glass of water first thing in the morning is one of the most loving, grace-filled ways to honor the body God gave you.

It doesn't need to be complicated. Room temperature. Warm if you like (and even better). Maybe with a squeeze of lemon if you're feeling fancy. Think of it as a holy rinse, washing away what's no longer needed, clearing out the internal fog, gently waking up your system so it can meet the day ready and steady. Here's what hydration does (besides making you feel like you've got your life together before 7:00 a.m.) supports digestion and metabolism, flushes toxins your body worked hard to process overnight, lubricates joints (your knees will thank you), boosts energy naturally (without the crash), and helps clear that first-thing-in-the-morning mental fog. What sometimes feels like hunger, crankiness, or fatigue may actually be your body's plea for water. This is rhythm. A small habit. A sacred yes, a holy, gentle start.

It's also not an anti-coffee campaign (I'd never betray my fave dark roast like that). I still enjoy my one cup, sometimes two. Now, I let the water come first, hydration before caffeination. It's a simple way to start the day from a place of nourishment and honor the relationship with your body and with the One who formed you from dust and breath and rivers of living water. Go ahead, pour the water; sip slowly and receive the day's grace. Then, by all means, fire up the coffee machine. (I'll meet you there).

Earth: Move with Gentle Intention

You were made for movement. Every time your muscles contract, healing happens. Muscle contraction is medicinal: it circulates blood, wakes up your lymphatic system, and signals your brain that you are alive, alert, and ready to engage. Your muscles, bones, and joints were created to work together in a holy collaboration. In the morning, gentle movement is one of the kindest ways to re-enter the world. You don't need to lace up running shoes or master a yoga flow. Just start small. Stretch your arms overhead while sitting on the edge of the bed. Roll your shoulders back and breathe deeply. Take a short walk outside, even if it's just to the mailbox. Stand in the light and sway for a minute to your breath. Movement is about connection, reminding your body, I'm still here. I'm still held. I'm still being renewed. One breath, one stretch, one step at a time.

Spiritually speaking, movement is prayer in motion. It's one way to honor the earth beneath your feet and the breath in your lungs. It's a reminder that faith isn't something that lives only in your head. It lives in your whole being. In every step, every stretch, every breath. Even five minutes of gentle movement can shift your energy. So, reach up, roll your shoulders, stand barefoot for a minute and feel the ground hold you.

A Pause: Talking Honestly About Our Bodies

Let's pause for a moment. We've been talking about waking up with the world around us. About getting back into your body. About moving slowly, breathing deeply, and noticing the holy rhythms that God built into how we're made. I want to name something. Maybe, as you read about caring for your body or paying attention to your breath, something inside you felt tight, or even a little uncomfortable. Maybe thinking about your body doesn't feel simple or easy. Maybe it feels tender. Or confusing. Or even a little painful.

If that's true for you, I want you to know you're not alone. Our bodies are more than muscles and bones. They carry stories. They hold memories. Some of those memories come from the world around us. Some come from childhood, from what people said or didn't say. Some come from culture, and sadly, some even come from the church. Sometimes, those messages hurt.

When we start talking about caring for our bodies as sacred gifts from God, it can bring up all kinds of feelings. Maybe you feel uncomfortable. Maybe a part of you wants to push this idea away. Or maybe you feel sad, because you've been through hard things that have made it tough to feel at home in your body. If you're feeling any of that, it's okay. It doesn't mean you're doing something wrong. It actually means you're paying attention. You're listening. And that's where healing begins, with gentle honesty and grace for the story your body holds.

I know this in my own body. I've heard that inner voice, the one that criticizes everything. Mine used to talk a lot (honestly, she still shows up sometimes). She always had something to say about how I looked, how I acted, and whether I was doing enough or being enough. She had strong opinions about how much space I should take up and usually she thought it was too much. Let's just say she wasn't exactly kind. Definitely not a cheerleader. Over time, I've learned that I don't have to let that voice run the show.

I've never fit into the world's idea of thin. For a long time, I let that define me. I let the scale measure more than just weight. I let it measure my worth. I truly believed that if my body looked different, then everything else would fall into place. I'd feel confident. I'd be accepted. I'd finally be enough. I didn't say that out loud, of course. I carried the lie that I had to shrink myself to be worthy.

For a long time, I held back because of how I felt about myself. I stayed quiet in meetings, even when I had good ideas. I second-guessed everything I said. Sometimes I avoided showing up altogether, certain that I didn't quite belong in the room, certain that others were more qualified, more worthy of being heard. I became an expert at disqualifying myself before anyone else had the chance to. The critic in my head had memorized the script, Stay small. Don't draw too much attention. Play it safe. Be nice. Be quiet. Be grateful you're even here.

Here's the hard truth: I believed that voice. Every word of it. I didn't question it, not for years, anyway. I just accepted those thoughts as facts, as if they were part of who I was. Just because I believed a lie for a long time doesn't make it true.

And that voice, the one that says you're not enough, not worthy, not lovable as you are, doesn't sound like Jesus. Not even close. The Jesus I know doesn't shame or shrink us. He doesn't demand we fix ourselves before we're worthy of love. He meets us in our mess, calls us by name, and reminds us that we are already enough, already deeply loved.

If that's been your story, if you've ever felt like you had to shrink yourself, prove yourself, or work harder just to be worthy, please hear this: Those are lies. That story you've been told, or the one you keep telling yourself over and over again, is not the story God tells about you. Jesus didn't stop halfway. Jesus went all the way through death, through pain, through every kind of human suffering to say this clearly and forever: You are already loved, already chosen and already enough because of who Jesus is and how deeply He loves you.

In Christ, there are no prerequisites for worthiness. It's not based on your pants size, your to-do list, your paycheck, or how many emails you answer. It's not about having it all together. It never was. You are already worthy because Jesus says so. Jesus defines your worth. Forever.

I know it's hard to really believe it. It's one thing to hear someone say, "You are enough." It's another thing to actually feel it deep inside. To live like it's true. Sometimes we know the right words in our heads while our hearts are still holding on to hurt. Shame can build big walls around our hearts so letting the truth in takes more than just hearing it once. It takes time. It takes practice. It takes formation, being reshaped by God's truth, over time, with love and patience. It's how we learn to live as if we really are already loved.

Theology gives us words to understand and talk about God's love. We need more than words. We need real-life help to live like God's truth is actually true. Jesus shows us how to live. His life was one of rhythm, prayer, intention, and deep connection to God. He never expected us to figure it all out alone. He gave us the gift of community as part of our formation. We need people: faithful, kind, Spirit-centered people who will accompany us. People who remind us who we are when we're feeling lost. People who will say, "Look again. Christ's light is still in you." Even when we can't feel it ourselves.

Because sometimes we just need someone to believe with us until we can believe again. We were never meant to experience life alone.

That's why I believe God put it on my heart to create the Breathing in Christ community. It's not a place where you'll be pushed to work harder or do more to prove your worth. It's a soft place to land; a sacred space for people who feel tired, stretched thin, or stuck in survival mode. Maybe that's been you too.

This community is for anyone learning to breathe again, not just with their lungs, but with their soul. It's for people who want to live from their Christ-given identity, not from burnout, busyness, or the pressure to have it all together. Here, we practice grace instead of perfection. We learn how to slow down, listen for God's voice, and return to the rhythm we were made for a life rooted in Jesus' love. I'll share more about that toward the end of this book. (If you're curious now, you can visit www.breathinginchrist.com).

For now, take a deep breath and remember: You don't have to fix yourself before you keep reading. You don't have to earn your place here. You don't have to try harder, do more, or have all the answers. Come as you are. Bring your questions. Bring your breath. Bring your whole self, even the parts that feel tired, unsure, or messy. There's room for all of it here. You are already enough because Jesus says you are. This is where we breathe again. Together.

Fire: Kindle Inner Focus with Stillness
There's a holy fire inside you. It might not feel like a big flame or a burning

passion, yet it's there, a spark placed in you by God on purpose. This flame doesn't demand attention. It doesn't shout. It waits. Warm, patient, ready to light the way back to who you are and Whose you are.

Fire doesn't keep burning all on its own. It needs to be tended. The same is true for the fire inside of us. When we pause, breathe, and make just a little space for stillness, that spark inside us comes back to life. It starts to glow again. Morning is a beautiful time to tend your soul. Throughout Scripture, fire is one of God's most powerful metaphors for holy presence.

There's Moses, barefoot on holy ground, drawn toward a bush that blazed with flame but wasn't consumed. From that fire, God spoke his name. There's the pillar of fire that led the Israelites through the wilderness, God's presence guiding them through uncertainty, offering light when the path ahead felt unknown. At Pentecost, the Spirit came like tongues of fire, igniting courage, connection, and purpose that turned a fearful room of followers into bold proclaimers of the gospel. Fire, in all these stories, reveals something about the nature of God: illuminating what's true, refining what needs to be released, comforting the weary, guiding the lost. That same flame, the Spirit of God, still burns today within you. This is why stillness in the morning matters. Making even the smallest space to remember the spark of God within you allows that holy fire to rise again, bringing warmth to your spirit to light the way.

Maybe that space looks like lighting a single candle while the sky is still waking up. One small flame can change the atmosphere of a room and your heart, reminding you the Holy Spirit is here, right now. Maybe it means opening your Bible and reading slowly. Just a few verses, maybe a single Psalm. One sentence that meets you right where you are. Or maybe you pick up a pen and you write a prayer. A simple prayer, a name you're carrying, a feeling you're sitting with, a question you want to ask God. Sometimes, it's simply sitting in the stillness, breathing deeply. Inhale: Come, Holy Spirit. Exhale: Here I am, Lord. No rush. Just breath and Jesus. This, too, is tending the flame. You don't have to fan the flame into a wildfire. Just tend to it, gently and consistently. Trust that Jesus meets you there, in the flicker, in the ordinary holy of morning light.

Midday Rhythm (10:00 a.m. - 2:00 p.m.) God's Energy in Motion

Midday has its own kind of energy. The sun is high, the day has found its stride and, biologically speaking, this is often your body's sweet spot. Around this time, your body is actually designed to feel more alert. Cortisol, your body's built-in "get-up-and-go" helper, is working to help you stay focused and motivated. Your brain may feel a little sharper now. You're not quite as sleepy as you were earlier, and you might find it easier to pay attention, solve problems, or check a few things off your to-do list. Even if you're not in full-on productivity mode, this part of the day often gives us a boost of clarity. It's a great time to work on a project or make an important decision.

Of course, not every day feels that smooth. Some days, midday comes with distractions, challenges, or a deep desire for a nap. Recognizing this rhythm can help us work with our body instead of against it. Midday is a good time to check in, physically, mentally, and spiritually, and ask, "Where is Jesus inviting me to focus right now? What matters most in this moment?"

Of course, "checking in" doesn't have to mean a 90-minute spiritual retreat or a perfectly peaceful lunch break with instrumental worship music in the background (though if that's your life, bless you, and please tell the rest of us your secrets). For the rest of us, here's what a midday check-in might look like:

Take a breath. Yep, just one to start. Inhale slowly through your nose. Exhale through your mouth like you're letting go of a sigh you've been holding since breakfast. Ask your body, "How are we doing?" You might be surprised at the answer. Tight shoulders? Clenched jaw? Stomach growling because lunch turned into coffee and a handful of crackers? Your body will tell you the truth if you pause long enough to listen. Ask your heart, "What do I need right now?" "Do I need a quick walk? A glass of water? To turn off the news for a minute? To step outside and remember God is God and I'm not?" Ask your spirit, "Where is Jesus in this moment?" Maybe Jesus is in the sunlight hitting your desk. Maybe in the quiet noise from the dishwasher. Maybe in the text you haven't responded to yet (the one from someone who needs your grace, or the one you need to reply to with your own gentle honesty).

These aren't fancy practices; however, they are powerful. They bring you back to the present moment, the only place you can actually notice Jesus, breathe deeply, and choose the next right thing. This part of the day is an opportunity to check in with yourself before your energy burns out completely.

I often think about the story in John 4, where Jesus stops at a well in the middle of the day. It's the hottest time, sun beating down, heat rising off the ground, the part of the day when most people are inside or resting. Jesus is out there, tired from walking, probably sweaty and hungry too. His disciples go off to find food, maybe falafel, maybe pita and hummus. We don't know exactly; we can imagine they were hoping for something filling and familiar. Meanwhile, Jesus stays behind. He doesn't rush ahead. He waits. Alone. Sitting in the quiet.

Then a Samaritan woman shows up. She's carrying a lot more than a water jar. She's carrying the weight of being judged, left out, and misunderstood. Her story is full of pain and silence, and she's used to avoiding people. That's probably why she comes to the well at noon, the hottest part of the day, when no one else is around. It's easier to deal with the heat than with the stares and whispers.

Jesus is there, waiting. On purpose. He's not in a hurry. Not multitasking. Not squeezing in a quick miracle between appointments. He stays. He notices her, and then Jesus speaks – gently, honestly, with dignity and curiosity, "Will you give me a drink?"

This moment at the well turns into one of the longest one-on-one conversations Jesus has in the entire Bible. Here's what's amazing: it's not with one of His disciples, with a priest, or a Bible expert. It's with her. A woman. A Samaritan. Someone most people at the time would have ignored or avoided. Not Jesus. Jesus sees her. Really sees her. He doesn't look away or talk down to her. He gives her time, attention, and dignity. While others might have dismissed her as unimportant or too broken, Jesus leans in and offers living water: hope, truth, and love that goes deeper than the well they're standing beside. This is what Jesus does. He shows up for the ones who feel forgotten and speaks life right into their story.

Midday gives us a chance to pause, just like Jesus did at the well. It's a time to stop and notice: Who or what is at my well right now? Maybe it's a coworker who needs a kind word. Maybe it's your own tired reflection in the mirror, asking for a little compassion. Or maybe, like that Samaritan woman, it's Jesus, waiting quietly, hoping you'll stop just long enough to breathe and notice Him.

The woman came to the well to get water. That was her plan. After talking with Jesus, she left her jar behind. Why? Because the thing she thought she needed most, water, wasn't what her heart needed most. What she truly needed was the presence of Jesus. Someone who really saw her. Someone who knew her story and still loved her.

You don't need to travel to an actual well to meet Jesus. (Although if standing by your kitchen sink with a glass of water is the closest thing, go with it!) Take just a moment, a quick pause, a deep breath to step out of the rush and remember you don't have to carry everything on your own.

Before you jump into the next task, what if you took a small pause? Stretch your legs. Step outside for a few minutes. Pour yourself a cool glass of water. Look out the window and pray, "Jesus, meet me here."

It's also this time of the day where midday hunger is real. It's easy to reach for whatever's fast, salty, or sweet. (Hello again, dark chocolate). What if lunch could be more than just a quick grab-and-go? What if it became a way to pause and connect with Jesus? Try this: choose something that feels alive. Something that reminds you it once grew, like an apple, a handful of carrots, a simple sandwich with fresh greens, or a bowl of warm soup that feels like a hug from the inside out. As you eat, bless your meal: "Jesus, thank You for this gift of nourishment." Yes, leftover pizza totally counts. This isn't about eating perfectly; it's about noticing Jesus in the middle of your day, even at the kitchen table or the office lunchroom. Lunch can be a small act of love – even your eating can be sacred.

Before returning from lunch, midday is another opportunity to move with gentleness. You don't need to break a sweat or go on a power walk (unless that sounds fun to you). This isn't about tracking your steps or checking off a workout. Take a few minutes to oxygenate your blood and muscles. Stretch your arms up toward the sky. Roll your shoulders a few times. Stand up and slowly walk to get a glass of water. Take a deep breath right at your desk. Walk a lap around your kitchen or stretch tall like you're reaching for the ceiling. That's it. That's enough. Movement reminds your soul: I'm here. I'm alive. I'm held.

You don't have to wait until the day is over to be renewed. Right here, in the middle of your ordinary life, Jesus is still offering living water. So, what's your practice? What will help you drink deeply today? Take a moment to ask your soul and listen for the holy invitation.

Afternoon (2:00 p.m. - 6:00 p.m.) The Sacred Slowdown

Ah, the afternoon. That magical stretch of the day where your brain starts thinking things like, "Just a quick nap," or "Wait. How is it only 2:17?" Tasks that felt easy in the morning now feel heavier, like walking through mud. Your to-do list is still sitting there, waiting. Your inbox is multiplying like loaves and fishes. Somewhere between answering emails and letting out your fourth big sigh, you realize you've been holding your breath. This part of the day is doing what it's meant to do. There's a natural dip in your energy built into the rhythm of how God created your body.

Your biology is trying to help you slow down. Around this time of day, your cortisol, the hormone that helps you stay alert, starts to drop and your blood sugar shifts. Your body gets quieter, slower, softer, whether or not you've scheduled time for that on your calendar. Most of us don't notice. Or if we do, we ignore it. We push through, chug more caffeine, scroll our phones, or grab a quick snack to keep going.

I used to push through this part of the day, too. I told myself it was "being strong" or "staying focused." I called it perseverance. Really, it was more like running on a mix of caffeine, sugar, and ignoring how tired I actually was. My favorite fix was a handful of chocolate-covered espresso beans (yep, dessert and energy all in one!) followed by a cold Coke Zero. It felt like a little celebration, a treat for being so responsible. Honestly, it did give me a boost – but only for about 30 minutes.

Then came the crash. My energy dropped and everything felt like a blur. By the time dinner rolled around, I was stuck in that weird in-between space of kind of hyper and also completely worn out. I wasn't rested. I wasn't focused. And I definitely wasn't present, not with my family, not with myself, and not with Jesus. I was going through the motions, doing what had to be done, hoping no one could tell how tired I really was.

At night, I'd climb into bed completely exhausted and somehow, still wide awake. I tried all the usual things: melatonin, a little magnesium, lavender oil on my pillow, even chamomile tea in a mug that said "Just Breathe." I gave sleep apps a try too. One time I accidentally ended up listening to a super serious botanist talk about how plants scream when they're stressed. (Not exactly the calm bedtime feel I was going for.) No matter what I tried, nothing really worked. The problem wasn't just that I couldn't fall asleep. The real issue was deeper. My body was tired, and my soul was restless. I needed more than a sleep hack, I needed rest that reached the heart.

The mid-afternoon slump is a built-in invitation to pause, to rest, to reset. You weren't made to sprint from morning 'til night without stopping. When we ignore our body's signals, we usually end up paying for it later. We feel it in all kinds of ways: we toss and turn at night; we lose our spark and creativity; we struggle to focus; we feel tense and stressed for no clear reason; we forget how to hear Jesus' voice saying, "You can rest now, my child."

You don't need to quit your job or throw your planner in the trash (even if that sounds kind of fun right now). Think of your body like a good friend. Would you yell at a friend for being tired? Of course not. You'd listen with kindness and care. The next time it's 3:00 in the afternoon and your brain feels fried, your energy has disappeared, and your hand is reaching for that third cup of coffee or another cookie without even thinking, pause for a second, take a deep breath, and ask yourself gently, "What do I really need right now?" You might be surprised by the answer.

One simple way to pause in the afternoon is to give yourself permission to rest, just for 10 to 15 minutes. If your schedule allows (or even if it doesn't but you know you really need a break), close your eyes. You don't have to fall asleep. Think of it as a holy pause. If you do drift off, that's okay too, it just means your body needs it. You can lie down if you're able or lean back in your chair. Unclench your jaw, allowing your shoulders to drop. Breathe in slowly. Breathe out a little longer than you breathe in. This kind of short rest is sometimes called "non-sleep deep rest" or NSDR. It can calm your body, lower stress, clear your mind, and help you return to your day more focused and peaceful. If it helps, set a gentle timer so you don't have to keep checking the clock. If your brain says, "You don't have time for this," gently answer, "I don't have time not to."

You can also try a focus reset. Ever feel like your brain has a bunch of tabs open at once and one of them is playing music and you can't figure out which one? That's your mind asking for a reset. When your thoughts feel jumbled or your attention is all over the place, one of the kindest things you can do is take a short break and give your brain a new signal: It's okay to pause.

Sometimes the best way to bring your focus back is to step away for a few moments and do something simple and kind for your mind and body. Try standing up from your screen and stretching, reach your arms overhead, roll your shoulders, or take a short walk around the room. That little bit of movement can make a big difference. You might light a candle and watch the flame dance. As you take three slow breaths, notice the light reminding you that Jesus' presence is always near, even in the small moments. If you can, open a window. Feel the breeze on your skin. Listen for the birds or even the sound of a lawn mower. These everyday sounds can help you feel grounded again.

If your space feels cluttered, take a minute to clear off a small corner of your desk or straighten a few things around you. Sometimes, making a little room outside helps make room inside.

Have you noticed how the voice in your head, the one that tells you you're not doing enough, gets louder in the afternoon? Just when your energy starts to dip, the inner critic shows up, ready to challenge you. "You should be further along," or "Why can't you focus?" When that critical voice shows up, try gently interrupting it. Take a deep breath and speak a kind, grounding truth out loud, something simple and honest, like: "I'm doing the best I can." "This moment is enough." "God is still with me." Remind yourself what's true; Jesus isn't keeping score. Jesus is holding you, right here, right now, just as you are.

By this time of day, most of us are sinking into our chairs like melted crayons. Our shoulders are hunched. Our necks are stretched forward. Our backs are curved like a tired plant leaning toward the last bit of sunlight. (Okay, maybe that's just me, but I'm guessing I'm not alone.) When your body feels crumpled and your energy's running low, it's a good time for a small reset. Nothing fancy. Just a moment of grace to realign your posture and your spirit.

Start by pausing whatever you're doing. Uncross your legs and place your feet flat on the floor. Sit tall, like the beloved child of God you are. Roll your shoulders back. Reach your arms overhead if it feels good. Take a deep, slow breath in. Then exhale fully, letting your body stretch into the space it was made to take up. As you breathe, you might offer a prayer, God, help me show up fully for what's left of this day. Or Holy Spirit, realign my posture and my heart.

There is quiet power in small resets; they're sacred spaces where Jesus meets you. Like little wells along your journey, they offer room to pause, to breathe, to simply be. Think of the Samaritan woman who came to the well tired and carrying a heavy heart. She didn't need to have it all together. She just showed up and Jesus was already there, waiting with kindness and living water. You can show up, too. Just as you are. Here, Jesus brings rest. Here, your soul is gently restored.

Evening (6:00 p.m. - 10:00 p.m.) Letting the Day Land Gently

Evenings are more than the tail end of the day. They are sacred ground. A gift from God meant to help you slow down, breathe deeply, and reconnect with yourself, with others, and with Jesus. It's not the time to see how much more you can squeeze in. It's the time to gently step out of "doing" and return to "being." The slow exhale of your day, evenings are your soft landing. A moment to look back and say, "Jesus, You've been with me today." A chance to let go of the day.

Can you imagine that there is no gold medal for Olympic-level evening multitasking? For the longest time, my evenings were a frantic juggling act. I'd be stirring dinner with one hand, answering emails with the other, while trying to switch the laundry, respond to texts, and maybe scroll through social media just long enough to lose track of what I was reheating, again. Sound familiar?

Across many cultures and spiritual traditions, there's a shared truth that your own body has probably been trying to tell you. How we spend our evenings deeply shapes how we rest, how we heal, and how we show up tomorrow. One of the biggest ways we throw off that evening rhythm is food. Yep, we're going there.

I'm talking about that late-night bowl of cereal. Or sneaking one more bite of lasagna after the kitchen's already clean. Or standing at the freezer with a spoon in the ice cream tub (no bowl necessary), or sipping straight from the bottle because, well, it's been that kind of day. No shame here. We've all done it. Often, we reach for food not because we're hungry, but because we're tired. Or stressed. Or sad. Or bored. Or looking for something to reward a long day. While there's absolutely room for treats and flexibility (grace always wins over guilt), it helps to ask ourselves gently, "What am I really craving right now?" Sometimes the answer is connection. Sometimes it's rest. Sometimes it's Jesus.

Here's something most of us don't think about – your body – the one God lovingly designed and called good, is doing more than just helping you get through the day. It's carrying the Holy Spirit. It's sacred space. Just like your soul needs rest, so does your body. When evening rolls in, your body starts to shift into its nighttime rhythm. Your brain is getting ready to rest, your heart rate slows, and even your digestion starts winding down. It's all part of the daily invitation to reset and restore.

When we toss in a heavy, late-night meal, when we snack on chips, grab seconds of mac and cheese, or munch our way through the pantry while watching TV, we're sending our body mixed signals. It's like telling someone to relax while handing them a long to-do list. Instead of getting to rest, your digestive system has to kick back into gear. It's trying to do the work of healing and restoring and processing that extra food at the same time. The result? You might sleep, but you probably won't feel rested. You might wake up groggy or achy or more tired than you were the night before. Often, we wonder why. After a full day of moving, thinking, caring, and doing, your body begins to shift into a quieter rhythm. The way you eat during this time can either support that sacred slowing or make it harder.

Long ago, "supper" wasn't just another word for dinner. It came from the same root as "soup," something simple, warm, and soothing. Supper was never meant to be complicated or heavy; it was meant to be a gentle close to the day. Perhaps we return to that idea. A warm bowl of broth. A light stew. A small plate of roasted vegetables, or a cup of marinated greens. A few slices of fresh fruit. These kinds of foods are easier for the body to receive and don't demand extra effort from your digestive system. Instead, they send a calming message: We're done striving now. You can rest. This kind of nourishment makes space for renewal and honors the quiet work your body is already doing as night draws near: healing, restoring, preparing you for tomorrow.

Evenings don't have to be about more: more noise, more rushing, more trying to get it all right. They can be about less. They can become a time of communing instead of consuming. When we release the pressure to create elaborate or time-consuming meals or chase some picture-perfect dinner, we create space for the people we love. Some of the most sacred dinners are the simplest ones. A warm bowl of soup. A piece of bread, still soft in the middle. A salad made with whatever is in the fridge. It's an invitation to trust that less really can be enough. Simple meals remind us that we don't need to impress anyone. We don't need to do more to be loved. Less really can be enough. Real fullness, the kind that satisfies your soul, comes from something deeper. It comes from Love. From knowing Jesus is at the table with you. When we simplify what we eat, we often feel more satisfied, not less. Love becomes the main course – the love you share with your body, the love you share with others.

This isn't about strict rules or about never eating late again. (I'm still saying yes to chips and guacamole after dinner once in awhile.) This is about listening to your body and noticing what helps it rest instead of wrestle. Evening is the moment to hand it all back to God. To say, "Here, Lord. I've carried what I could. Now I place it in Your hands."

Beyond food, there are other ways to encourage your body to slow down. As the sun goes down, your body naturally starts to wind down too. You can help it along by dimming the lights around you. Turn off bright overhead lights and switch to soft lamps or light a candle. Bright lights can feel loud, signaling your home is still in "go mode." Softer lighting tells your body, "It's okay to slow down now." This small change helps your mind and heart find a sense of peace.

A gentle walk is, as you've probably guessed by now, great any time of day. This time of day, a slow walk can help your body exhale the day. You don't have to go far, just down the block or around the yard is enough. As the cool air touches your face, look up at the sky and listen to the sounds of evening. This is less about fitness and exercise, and far more about walking away from the hurry, one step at a time.

Evening can be a beautiful time to reach out to someone who matters to you. Sit down with your family for a few minutes. Call a friend or send a short voice message. Even a simple text that says, "I'm thinking of you" can go a long way. When we connect with someone safe and kind, it helps us remember that we're not walking through life alone. These small touches of love can soften the rough parts of the day and bring comfort to a tired heart.

As the day winds down, your soul needs space to shift from all the noise into quiet. Another helpful way to do that is by stepping away from your screens. If you can, turn off your phone, tablet, or TV about an hour before bed. If that feels like too much right now, even 20 minutes can make a difference. Try replacing screen time with something calmer – like reading a book, listening to soft music, or just sitting in stillness. This digital pause allows your brain to take a break from the headlines, messages, and scrolling and gives your heart room to breathe in Christ as the last thing you take in for the night.

As you've learned by now, your body and mind love rhythm. When something happens regularly, at about the same time and in the same way, your body starts to learn what to expect. That's why bedtime routines can be so helpful. It doesn't really matter what your bedtime routine looks like. What matters most is that you do it with kindness and do it consistently. Over time, even simple habits can help your nervous system shift gears and settle into rest.

You might try turning the bed down and lighting a candle. You could read a short verse from the Bible or enjoy quiet time in prayer. Maybe you write down three things you're thankful for in a journal or on a scrap of paper. You might take a few deep breaths and ask yourself, "Where did I feel close to Jesus today? Where did I feel disconnected? Where do I need Jesus to meet me with grace?" Water has a quiet kind of power. Whether it's a warm shower, a long bath, or even just washing your face slowly at the sink, this can become more than a routine, it can be a holy moment. As the water touches your skin, take a deep breath and say in your heart, "Jesus, wash away what I don't need to carry anymore. Get me ready for rest." Whatever you choose, try to keep it simple and peaceful. Your day is done and God is holding you through the night.

You don't have to try every practice. It's simply an invitation to begin. Choose just one thing that feels possible tonight. Something small. Listen to what your body is saying and trust what your spirit needs. Tomorrow will come, full of its own needs and noise. For now, allow the day to rest. Allow your heart to rest. Allow God to hold what's left undone.

Night (10:00 p.m. - 2:00 a.m.) Rest and Digest

By the time your head hits the pillow and the world outside starts to quiet down, something amazing is just getting started inside your body. Even though it feels like you're just lying still, your body is doing some of its most important work while you sleep. Between about 10:00 p.m. and 2:00 a.m., your body begins to restore itself. Muscles repair. Organs rest and recharge. Your brain starts sorting through the day, clearing away clutter and storing memories. It's called the "Rest and Digest" time, your built-in overnight wellness plan.

When you go to bed with your body feeling calm and gently nourished, instead of full or heavy from a big, late-night meal, your body can fully enter its nighttime rhythm, the one God designed to heal and restore you. During this time, your body quietly gets to work, cleaning out waste from your cells and balancing important hormones that help with mood, energy, and rest. It refills what's been used up during the day, kind of like recharging a battery. Your organs, especially your liver, play a big role in this. All day long, they've been busy keeping you going. At night, they finally get a chance to reset, to filter out what your body doesn't need, and to prepare you for a new day.

This is the grace of the overnight hours: while you sleep, God keeps working. God's design takes over, healing, restoring, and renewing you from the inside out. Here are a few gentle, grace-filled evening practices to help your body and spirit lean into rest and digest:

Your bedroom can become a peaceful space where your body and spirit know, "This is where I'm safe. This is where I can rest." You don't need fancy furniture or perfect decorations. What matters most is how the room feels to you. Is it calm? Is it quiet? Does it make you breathe a little easier when you walk in? Most of us sleep better in a room that's cool, dark, and quiet. A fan, blackout curtains, or a soft nightlight can help create that gentle space. Also notice what's around you.

Try clearing off that one chair with the pile of clothes or putting away a few things that feel distracting or stressful. Add textures that make you feel comforted. A soft blanket. Sheets that feel cozy. A pillow that supports your neck just right. Maybe add a calming scent, like lavender, on your pillow or in a diffuser. Your body will begin to recognize these small signals as a cue to slow down and rest. You could also place something nearby that reminds you of God's love – a short Bible verse, a breath prayer, or a small cross.

While we've talked about what we eat before bed, it's helpful to understand the best times to eat before bed. When you stop eating about 2 to 3 hours before bedtime, you give your digestive system a break. That might sound simple, but it's a big deal. Instead of working hard to break down food, your body can shift into healing mode. It starts cleaning out toxins, fixing tired cells, balancing your hormones, and refilling what you've used up during the day. That's why lighter evening meals can make a big difference. When we eat with this kind of care, we support the holy work that happens through the night. We rest better. We heal better. And we wake up feeling more like ourselves.

Gratitude doesn't keep us up at night. You know what often does? Worry. Worry about tomorrow. Regrets from the day. That one conversation you wish had gone differently. Even the quiet can feel loud when your mind won't settle down. Instead of focusing on what didn't get done or what you wish you could change, try shifting your heart toward gratitude. As you lie in bed, try letting your last thoughts be thank-you prayers.

Thank You, Jesus, for the laughter at dinner. Thank You for that text from a friend. Thank You for the sunlight that warmed my face this morning. Thank You for carrying me through today, even when I felt like I was barely holding on. Simple prayers of thanks become soft, steady breaths. Each one helps your body relax and your heart feel a little lighter. When you say thank you to Jesus, out loud or in your thoughts, you are inviting a peaceful night's rest and space to hear Jesus say, I've got this. You can rest now.

Early Morning (2:00 a.m. - 6:00 a.m.) Restoring

These are the softest hours of the day. The sky outside is dark and the world has gone quiet. Even your house, hopefully, is still. In that calm, your breath begins to slow, matching the peaceful rhythm of the night. This is sacred time. As you curl up under your covers, maybe in your favorite pajamas, maybe with a soft blanket or your go-to pillow, your body goes to work healing and restoring what the day has taken. This stretch of night is when your body gets its deepest rest. While you are asleep, your muscles are knitting themselves back together, cell by cell. Your immune system is strengthening its defense team. Your brain is busy tidying the mental clutter: filing memories, clearing out the junk drawer of stress, integrating the stories of your day like a Spirit-led librarian with a purposeful plan.

All of this goodness happens quietly while you sleep. No one sees it. These nighttime hours are where some of God's most beautiful healing happens. This is the space where tomorrow begins, like the soft soil before a seed sprouts. These early morning hours are the womb of a new day, where God is already at work shaping what's next – while you rest.

And yes, sometimes this rhythm doesn't go perfectly. Maybe you stayed up too late watching just one more episode. Maybe a text came in, and you felt like you had to answer. Maybe your mind started racing before the sun came up. Or maybe the dog, the toddler, or your own thoughts decided that 3:00 a.m. was a great time to have a little party. It happens. Life happens.

Our bodies are beautifully human, not machines. Rhythms bend. Some nights are smooth, others are anything but. Even when things don't go as planned, grace remains. You're still held. You can always begin again the next night or even the next breath.

Jesus in Every Hour

We've walked through a full day together. Hour by hour. Breath by breath. From the early light of morning to the busy hours of the afternoon. From the slow evening wind-down to the deep rest of night. Each part of the day holds something special. Each one is an invitation to pause, to notice, and to remember Jesus is here. This chapter is your reminder that every hour matters. Your body, your breath, your energy, they're part of how God made you. They're signals, teachers, holy ground. They help you listen to what your soul really needs.

Before moving on, take a moment to pause right here. The next few questions are here to help you notice what your daily rhythms really feel like. You don't have to rush through them or answer them all at once. Maybe one will speak to you today. Maybe another will come back to you later this week. Consider these questions an open conversation between you and Jesus – a quiet way to listen to what the Spirit might be whispering underneath the busyness of life. Discovering a life of Breathing in Christ is about gently coming back, again and again, to a rhythm of grace. A way of living that reminds you how much you are loved and that you can begin again anytime.

Reflection: Listening to the Rhythm of Your Life

When during my day do I feel most alive, most awake, or most at peace? When do I feel the most tired, restless, or disconnected?

How is my body speaking to me lately, through yawns, tight shoulders, hunger, headaches, or shortness of breath? Am I paying attention with kindness, or pushing through without noticing?

Are there parts of my day where I feel like I'm moving with God's rhythm? Are there moments where I might be going against it because of habit, pressure, or trying to keep up?

Which parts of my daily routine feel good for my soul, filling me up? Which parts leave me feeling drained or stressed?

What is my breath like during the day? Am I holding it without realizing? Rushing? Or letting it bring me back to Jesus, slowly and gently?

Where could I add one small pause, a breath prayer, a slow step outside, a quiet moment to notice Jesus' presence? Which parts of my day feel shaped by what the world expects from me? Which parts feel shaped by grace?

If I really believed my body was a beautiful, beloved creation, fearfully and wonderfully made, how might that change how I treat it? How I eat, move, rest, or breathe?

What's one small shift I could try this week to live more in step with the rhythm God already placed inside me?

Interlude
A Simple Invitation from Creation to Nourish

EVEN WHEN LIFE feels busy or far from peaceful, God's creation still offers us healing. Our bodies remember what we were made for: sunlight on our skin, cool air in our lungs, fresh food from the earth. We were created for connection. For rhythm. For nourishment that comes from the world God so lovingly made.

In earlier chapters, we explored how breath, energy, cravings, and daily choices are shaped by how closely we live with God and how closely we live with creation. Now, this section invites you into the kitchen to prepare simple, grounding meals that align with the sacred rhythm already inside you.

These recipes are not fancy. You don't need a chef's kitchen or a long grocery list. What helps most is setting up your kitchen with love and intention:

Keep a few basic whole foods on hand: vegetables, grains, beans, leafy greens, nuts, and fruits.

Visit a local farmer's market, when possible, for fresh produce and for the reminder that food is grown, not made.

Stock your pantry with simple staples: olive oil, garlic, lentils, oats, seeds, broths, and herbs.

Think simple and freedom; these are creation rhythms to receive.

The recipes that follow are meant to nourish your body while gently supporting your spirit. They honor God's good creation and remind us that food can be more than fuel, it can be sacred. With each bite, receive the gift that you are sustained, you are loved, and you are part of creation's beautiful design.

Sunrise Oats (warm & grounding) A nourishing, fiber-rich way to begin the day.
   1/2 cup rolled oats
   1 cup water or plant-based milk
   1/2 grated apple or mashed banana

Dash of cinnamon
1 tbsp walnuts or sunflower seeds
Simmer oats in liquid until soft (5 to 10 minutes). Stir in fruit, cinnamon, and nuts.

Berry Blessing Bowl (vibrant & joyful) Quick, energizing, and antioxidant rich.
1/2 cup plain yogurt (or coconut or Greek yogurt)
1/2 cup berries (fresh or frozen)
1 tbsp chia seeds
Drizzle of honey or maple syrup
Sprinkle of granola or crushed almonds
Layer in a bowl and enjoy without scrolling!

Green Glow Smoothie Start your morning with energy and clarity.
1 handful spinach or kale
1 banana
1/2 avocado
1/2 cup frozen pineapple or mango
1 tbsp chia or flax seeds
1 cup water or almond milk
Blend until smooth, breathing in gratitude and sipping slowly.

Cinnamon Apple Quinoa Bowl (warm and protein-rich)
1/2 cup cooked quinoa
1/2 apple, diced
Dash of cinnamon and nutmeg
1 tsp maple syrup
Splash of almond milk or coconut milk
Warm gently and stir together.

Avocado Toast with Greens (grounding & energizing)
1 slice whole grain or sourdough bread, toasted
1/2 avocado, mashed
Handful of arugula or baby spinach
Pinch of sea salt, drizzle of olive oil

Hearty Lentil & Rice Bowl (filling and balancing)
1/2 cup cooked brown rice (or other grain of your choosing)
1/2 cup cooked lentils
Roasted zucchini, carrots, or mushrooms (or other veggies of choice)
Tahini drizzle or splash of balsamic or other favorite dressing.

Mid-Afternoon Soul Smoothie (light & uplifting)
1 banana
1/2 cup berries
1 tbsp hemp seeds or flax
1/2 cup plain yogurt or plant-based milk.

Midday Reset Salad (light and cleansing) Perfect for a nourishing break between tasks.
>2 cups mixed greens
>1/2 cucumber, sliced
>1/4 avocado
>1 boiled egg or scoop of chickpeas
>Olive oil + lemon juice drizzle
>Pinch of sea salt and cracked pepper
>Toss gently and enjoy slowly!

Holy Hummus Wrap (portable & peaceful) Balanced and simple, satisfying without slowing you down.
>1 whole grain wrap
>2 tbsp hummus
>Sliced cucumber, shredded carrots, greens
>Dash of turmeric or cumin
>Roll & cut.

Creation Bowl Lunch A rainbow of healing in one bowl.
>1/2 cup cooked quinoa or brown rice
>1/2 cup roasted sweet potato or squash
>1/2 cup sautéed greens (kale, chard, or spinach)
>1/4 avocado, sliced
>Handful of chickpeas or black beans
>Drizzle of olive oil, lemon, and sea salt.

Simple Chickpea Salad (quick & nourishing)
>1/2 cup chickpeas
>1/2 tomato, diced
>Cucumber slices
>Olive oil + lemon juice
>Pinch of sea salt and parsley
>Mix in a bowl and serve chilled or at room temp.

Garden Snack Plate (mindful & grounding) A gentle reset between meals.
>Handful of cherry tomatoes
>1 sliced cucumber (or any other accessible green veggies)
>A few olives or a cheese slice
>5 - 7 almonds or cashews
>Arrange with beauty and enjoy.

Healing Carrot Ginger Soup Bright, warm, and calming for the digestive system.
>1 tbsp olive oil
>1 small onion, chopped
>1 lb carrots, peeled and sliced
>1 tbsp fresh ginger, grated
>3 cups vegetable broth

Salt and pepper to taste
Sauté onion in oil until soft. Add carrots, ginger, and broth. Simmer until carrots are tender. Blend until smooth.

Zucchini Basil Soup Gentle and green; soothing on summer nights or when your body needs something light.
1 tbsp olive oil
2 zucchinis, chopped
1 small onion, chopped
2 cups vegetable broth
Handful of fresh basil
Salt to taste
Sauté zucchini and onion until soft. Add broth and simmer for 10 minutes. Blend with basil until creamy.

Golden Lentil & Coconut Soup Comforting, anti-inflammatory blend that's both grounding and gentle.
1 tbsp coconut oil or olive oil
1/2 cup red lentils
1 carrot, diced
1 clove garlic
1/2 tsp turmeric
3 cups water or vegetable broth
1/2 cup canned coconut milk
Salt to taste
Sauté garlic, carrot, and turmeric. Add lentils and broth. Simmer until the lentils are soft (about 20 minutes). Stir in coconut milk.

Simple Miso Soup Mineral-rich and grounding, ideal when your stomach needs a break but your soul needs comfort.
2 cups water
1 tbsp miso paste
1/2 cup diced tofu (optional)
A few pieces of seaweed or chopped spinach
Chopped green onions
Warm the water but don't boil. Stir in miso until dissolved. Add remaining ingredients and heat gently.

Potato Leek Soup A classic, creamy without the cream; earthy, simple, and satisfying.
1 tbsp olive oil or butter
2 leeks, sliced (white and light green parts only)
2 to 3 potatoes, peeled and chopped
3 cups vegetable broth
Salt and pepper
Sauté leeks until soft. Add potatoes and broth. Simmer until potatoes are tender. Blend until smooth or leave rustic.

Roasted Root Medley (grounding & earthy) Great for a warm, simple evening meal.
   1 carrot, 1 parsnip, 1 small sweet potato, chopped
   Toss with olive oil, rosemary, and sea salt
   Roast at 400°F for 25 to 30 mins
   Serve with a spoonful of lentils or quinoa.

Restorative Evening Soup Gentle on digestion, calming for body and soul.
   1 tbsp olive oil
   1/2 onion, chopped
   2 carrots, chopped
   2 celery stalks, chopped
   1 clove garlic
   4 cups vegetable broth
   1/2 cup lentils or barley
   Handful of greens (spinach or parsley)
   Sauté onion, carrots, celery, and garlic until soft. Add broth and lentils and simmer
   for 30 minutes. Add greens at the end. Serve warm with gratitude.

Evening Sweet Potato Mash (soothing & simple)
   1 baked sweet potato
   1 tsp ghee or olive oil
   Sprinkle of cinnamon and sea salt
   Mash together and serve warm.

Warm Cinnamon Apples A grounding treat that fills you with comfort.
   2 apples, sliced
   1 tsp cinnamon
   1 tsp coconut oil or butter
   Optional: dash of maple syrup or honey
   Sauté apples in oil or butter over low heat with cinnamon until tender. Drizzle
   with maple syrup, if desired.

Baked Banana with Almond Butter Creamy, warm, and satisfying. A hug in dessert
form.
   1 ripe banana
   1 tbsp almond or peanut butter
   Optional: sprinkle of cinnamon or crushed nuts
   Slice banana lengthwise, add almond butter, and bake at 350°F for 10 minutes.

Chia Pudding with Berries Rich in fiber and omega-3s and it feels like a treat.
   3 tbsp chia seeds
   1 cup almond or oat milk
   1/2 tsp vanilla
   Handful of fresh or frozen berries
   Mix chia seeds with milk and vanilla. Refrigerate for at least 1 hour (or overnight).
   Top with berries.

Peaceful Pear Snack (gentle & sweet)
    1 ripe pear, sliced
    Sprinkle of cinnamon
    1 tbsp almond butter for dipping.

Honey-Lavender Yogurt Bowl Cooling and calming for the nervous system.
    1/2 cup plain Greek or plant-based yogurt
    1 tsp honey
    A pinch of culinary lavender or a few edible flowers
    Optional: a spoonful of granola or chopped pistachios
    Stir honey and lavender into yogurt. Add toppings.

Almond-Date Energy Bites (sweet & sustaining)
    1/2 cup almonds
    4 or 5 pitted dates
    1 tbsp chia seeds
    Dash of cinnamon
    Splash of vanilla extract
    Pulse in a food processor until sticky. Roll into small balls. Keep refrigerated.

Lemon Ginger Cooked Water (morning or evening) Supports digestion and warms the body gently.
    1 slice fresh ginger
    1–2 lemon slices
    2 cups water
    Simmer on the stove for 10 minutes.

Chamomile Lavender Night Water (bedtime ritual) A calming sleep aid to end the day in peace.
    1 chamomile tea bag
    1 drop food-grade lavender oil or a pinch of dried lavender
    1 cup hot water
    Steep for 5 to 7 minutes. Drink slowly under soft lighting.

Golden Glow Tea (inflammation support & warmth)
    2 cups water
    1/4 tsp turmeric + pinch black pepper
    Small slice of fresh ginger
    Optional: 1 tsp honey
    Simmer for 10 minutes.

Chapter 4
Vine & The Branches

I'VE ALWAYS LOVED the imagery of the vine and the branches which Jesus uses in John 15. Showing us just how close Jesus wants to be, it's one of the most personal and loving pictures Jesus gives us. "Abide in me, as I abide in you. Just as the branch cannot bear fruit by itself unless it abides in the vine, neither can you unless you abide in me. I am the vine, you are the branches."

The Greek word Jesus uses here, μένω (menō), means to remain, to stay, to endure, to make your home. Jesus is saying, "Make your home in me, just like I make my home in you." Jesus is inviting us to settle in, to stay close, to live our lives deeply connected to Him. This is the language of belonging, of being rooted and knowing we're not alone.

To the people listening to Jesus, the image of a vine would have been immediate and vivid. Vineyards were part of everyday life in ancient Israel. In the Hebrew Scriptures, the vine had long symbolized Israel itself, God's chosen people, meant to bear good fruit in the world. The prophets spoke of Israel as a vine that had gone wild or barren, one that failed to produce the fruit of justice, mercy, and faithfulness (see Isaiah 5 and Psalm 80). So when Jesus stood among his disciples and said, "I am the true vine," Jesus was declaring that He, not the temple system or ethnic lineage, was now the source of true life and identity. In Jesus, a new kind of vineyard was growing.

Vines were a sign of God's blessing and a staple of life. A healthy vine meant harvest, wine, community, and joy. The vine was a symbol of life lived together. We see the power of this at the very beginning of Jesus' public ministry, at the wedding in Cana (John 2). It's no accident that Jesus' first miracle involves wine, the fruit of the vine, and a celebration. When the wine runs out, so does the joy and hospitality of the gathering. Jesus steps in to reveal something deeper: that Jesus is the source of true abundance. What Jesus provides is better than what came before. The vine, then, becomes a symbol of God's desire for us to live in this same connection and shared joy. Through the Vine, Jesus turns scarcity into abundance and invites us into a life that overflows with grace. Jesus' words in John 15 reframe the entire meaning of what it means to belong to God; Jesus is the vine, we are the branches. Jesus is describing a connection that is life-giving and deeply rooted in care. To abide in Jesus is to be rooted in Jesus' life and love.

Vines don't thrive on sentiment alone. For a branch to stay healthy and bear fruit, a great deal of effort must go into keeping the vine healthy. Growth comes through cultivated, intentional care. In biblical times, tending a vine was a hands-on, intentional process that required daily care and deep familiarity with the plant. A skilled vine keeper would walk through the vineyard regularly, inspecting each branch for signs of disease, overgrowth, or dryness. The branches would be carefully pruned to remove the parts of the plant that would drain life or hinder fruitfulness, to ensure the roots stayed nourished. Watering was done with attention to timing and need, ensuring the roots stayed nourished without flooding them. The soil around the vines was often tilled and cleared of weeds to keep the vine from being choked out.

Vines were also trained to grow along a trellis or wall so they would not sprawl on the ground and be exposed to rot, pests, or damage. They didn't grow wild in random soil. They weren't left to nature's whim. If you've ever walked through a vineyard, you'll notice wooden frames or wires that the vines grow along. The trellis trains the vine to grow in a direction that allows sunlight and air to reach every leaf. It doesn't force growth, it supports it. Without the trellis, the vine can tangle or grow wild, its fruit lying vulnerable on the ground. The health of the vine was the result of a long, loving partnership between the vine and the one who tended it. The people listening to Jesus would've known this. They lived among vineyards. They understood the long, slow process of tending to the soil, pruning the branches, and waiting patiently for fruit. They knew the importance of pruning as purposeful care. They understood the waiting; fruit doesn't ripen in a day. Growing grapes meant committing to the long haul. You had to tend the vine consistently, even when it looked like nothing was happening.

Just as vines needed daily attention in ancient times, our spiritual lives need intentional care. Growth doesn't happen by accident. It occurs, over time, through rhythms of connection, pruning, and patience. Our souls, like vines, need healthy soil, steady nourishment, and space to grow. This means creating environments, internal and external, where the life of Christ can flow freely. Like a trellis supports a vine, our spiritual habits can gently guide our lives in a direction that allows light and grace to reach us. Just as a vine can't force fruit to appear overnight, we can't force transformation. We can stay connected. We can let go of the frantic pace and instead choose rhythms that keep us rooted in love.

And yes, pruning comes. There are seasons when we're invited to release what's no longer life-giving: habits, roles, or rhythms that may have once served us but now hinder our growth. It's part of being loved by a faithful Gardener who sees what we're capable of becoming. In every season, Jesus remains our Vine. Our call is simply to abide. This is how we respond to the love Jesus has already offered, by staying close to the One who has already called us His own.

Spiritual Practice
Tending the Vine

Set aside 10 to 15 minutes in a quiet space. Begin with a few slow, deep breaths. Imagine yourself as a branch connected to the Vine, Christ, secure, supported, and nourished.

Reflect:

Where in your life do you feel most connected to Jesus right now?

Where do you feel tangled, dry, or disconnected?

Is there a habit, responsibility, or mindset that may need to be gently pruned?

What small habit or rhythm could serve as a trellis supporting your connection to Jesus this week?

Living From Connection
Apart from me, you can do nothing.

Jesus certainly does not mince words in John 15:5 when He says, "Apart from me, you can do nothing." Our purpose is to stay close to Jesus. Abide in Him. That's it. This is clear. Crystal clear. Yes, there remain other deep mysteries about God. This part is simple. Abide in me. Stay with me. It's a sobering and freeing truth all at once. Sobering because we often try to do so much without ever pausing to root ourselves in Christ. Freeing because it means we're not the source of the fruit. We're not the vine. We're the branches.

One of my core convictions, if you haven't picked up on it by now, is that experiencing Jesus in an exhausting world asks us to show up to the relationship. The invitation is already on the table. Any relationship that matters to us, our life partner, our children, our closest friends, requires more than occasional attention. It asks for intentional time and a willingness to stay close, even when life gets loud or difficult. Our relationship with Jesus is no different; it's our center, the vine, the source. If we want to experience Jesus, not just talk about Jesus, we make space to notice and be with Him. We want to be where life flows, where our soul can breathe.

We prioritize what we value – our actual, ordinary, messy lives – around staying connected to Jesus. Our lives are always being shaped by what we say yes to. What we say yes to is a reflection of what we treasure. This is your opportunity to begin building rhythms around what's most life-giving rather than what's loudest or most urgent. This is where abiding happens because everything we truly need flows from there.

Tending To Your Growing Conditions

We're all growing toward something. The question isn't if we're growing, it's what we're growing toward and how we're being shaped along the way. Even the most beautiful branch can wither if the soil is dry or ignored. What allows a branch to thrive is not only about the vine, it's also about what surrounds it. The soil matters. The environment matters. The conditions that nurture our roots – our mindset, our choices, our rhythms, our community – all shape the kind of fruit our lives will bear. We often want to rush ahead to the fruit, yet lasting growth always begins underground.

Our lives are being formed by the environments we choose or don't choose. By the voices we listen to. The habits we repeat. The spaces we inhabit. The beliefs we hold. We are shaped by what we do regularly and what we allow to root in us. Without care, we can start growing in directions that tangle and exhaust us rather than help us abide.

With Jesus as the Vine and God as the Master Gardener, we are invited to participate in cultivating the environment that supports abiding. Our beliefs, habits, rhythms, and choices are like sunlight, water, and nutrients. While they don't create growth on their own, they make growth possible. We are going to consider five elements every healthy branch needs, with gentle questions to help you tend to them.

Light

Again Jesus spoke to them, saying, "I am the light of the world. Whoever follows me will never walk in darkness but will have the light of life." - (John 8:12)

Light is essential for growth. Light helps us see clearly. In our spiritual lives, light is the presence of Christ that reveals truth and helps us walk in clarity. Not all light is the same. Some things may appear bright and shiny yet ultimately leave us drained or distracted. Jesus offers a light that leads to life.

What lights up your soul with joy, clarity, and hope?
Where are you noticing God's truth gently illuminating something in you?

Water

Jesus told the woman at the well, "Whoever drinks the water I give them will never thirst." (John 4:14). Water is the source of refreshment and renewal. Spiritually, we all need soul-deep hydration, truth that quenches something in our hearts. Without water, we become dry, brittle, and reactive. Jesus offers living water that satisfies the thirst beneath our doing. Jesus invites us to drink from him.

What helps your soul feel nourished and refreshed?

Are there daily or weekly rhythms that leave you feeling spiritually hydrated?

Soil

In the parable of the sower, Jesus describes seeds falling on different types of soil. Some shallow, some rocky, some full of thorns, and some rich and ready. (Luke 8:4-15)

Your soil is the belief system underneath your habits, your inner dialogue, and your sense of worth. Healthy soil feeds your growth. If your inner soil is packed with perfectionism, shame, or unexamined lies, it can stunt your growth. Beliefs about Jesus, yourself, and what makes life meaningful all live here.

What are some of the things you believe about yourself and God?
What's one thought or belief you'd like to bring to Jesus and ask, "Is this really true?"

Pruning

"He removes every branch in me that bears no fruit. Every branch that bears fruit he prunes to make it bear more fruit." (John 15:2)

Pruning is care; a gardener prunes to protect and strengthen the vine. Sometimes what needs to go isn't "bad," it's simply too much. We all accumulate clutter – mental, spiritual, emotional – distractions, comparisons, even good things that have grown out of proportion. Pruning is a gift and makes room for what matters most to grow with intention.

What's weighing you down or pulling your attention away from what matters?

Is there something you've outgrown – or something that's outgrown its place?

Trellis

A trellis supports the growth that's already happening. In the same way, spiritual practices, community, and healthy rhythms, hold us up as we grow in Jesus. A trellis helps a vine receive sunlight and air, preventing it from collapsing under its own weight. We need structures that lift us into openness and connection, with habits and support systems that guide.

What practices help you stay connected to Christ?
Do you have a rhythm of rest, prayer, or community that supports your growth?

Choosing Alignment Over Acceleration

In behavior change theory, meaningful growth is about why and how consistently we do it. Speed without clarity leads to burnout while clarity of direction makes our actions sustainable. Behavior change research tells us that change sticks when it flows from identity. In other words, we don't just build habits to improve, we build habits to live into who we believe we are. Our identity is rooted in grace, in being branches of the Vine.

Healthy vines grow in response to care. In the life of faith, action flows from listening, rather than rushing to fix. Still, the urge to leap into doing is real. As soon as we notice what feels out of rhythm, we're ready to overhaul everything. I'll wake up earlier. I'll restructure my whole week. I'll finally stick to that meal plan, drink more water than a camel, and read through the entire Bible this year, chronologically, of course. We might be tempted to grab a metaphorical shovel and start digging, determined to fix what's broken – immediately. Abiding begins with listening for what Jesus is already doing in you. Clarity comes from hearing Jesus.

In the life of abiding, there's a holy space that often gets overlooked. It's the space between noticing and doing. In the language of faith, we call this space discernment. Like a sacred pause, a place of listening before leaping, or what I refer to as a trellis moment, where we let Jesus gently guide the direction of our growth before we start climbing.

When we notice something that feels off, our first impulse is often to fix it. Rearrange. Solve. Do something. Discernment invites us to slow down long enough to ask deeper questions: What is God inviting me into in this season? Where is love leading me? What fruit is Jesus cultivating in me, and what might need to be pruned?

Just like healthy vines are tended with care, discernment invites us to pause and tend to what we've noticed in our own lives. Our weariness. Our desires. The habits we fall into. Instead of rushing to fix or produce, discernment asks us to linger. To sit with Jesus long enough for clarity to take root. Before we rearrange our calendar, sign up for something new, or try to overhaul everything in a weekend, we ask a deeper question: Is this a season to plant, to prune, to rest, or to rise? This is the heart of discernment, listening for what Jesus is already doing in us. Because sometimes fruit is already growing, just beneath the surface, and we simply need to wait and water. We ask for wisdom. We ask Jesus to show us the kind of fruit that matters: peace, joy, patience, gentleness, faithfulness. Fruit that lasts.

Reflection Questions

What am I noticing in my life right now? (Energy levels, emotions, patterns, or longings?)

Where do I feel disconnected, rushed, reactive, or depleted? What might that disconnection be trying to show me?

What fruit do I long to see in my life and what small choices might help it grow? (Peace, joy, patience, presence, courage…)

What season am I in right now: planting, pruning, resting, or rising? How might Jesus be inviting me to tend to this season with grace?

Chapter 5
Living Sacred in the Everyday

TIME IS THE river carrying our life forward. Every choice we make, every breath we take, and every habit we keep happens inside that flow. The way we fill our hours tells others what we care about, who we rely on, and why we believe we're here. Time is the very medium through which our lives unfold.

Where Your Time Goes, Life Follows

God designed time in rhythm (not with alarm clocks or to-do lists). Genesis shows this holy rhythm: "And there was evening, and there was morning … the first day." God could have spoken the universe into being all at once; instead, God chose rhythm. One step at a time. One movement at a time. One day at a time. This tells us something essential. God made time as something to be received with an openness to honor and be lived fully.

Just like there is day and night, work and rest, doing and being, our lives were meant to move with that same gentle pattern. When we fall out of sync, our bodies, minds, and spirits feel it. We get tired, anxious, and distracted and we start living like every second has to be packed with something. Instead of noticing the moment we're in, we just try to survive it. That's when we know it's time to return – to slow down and remember the rhythm that God wrote into our very breath.

Every day we are making choices: what to focus on, who to listen to, how to spend our energy. All of those choices happen inside time. That's why how we live our time is how we live our life. When you take time to listen to a friend, you're living out love. When you pause to pray, you're saying, "Jesus, this moment matters." Time is something we live inside of and shapes our experiences – how we feel, how we relate to others, and how we connect with God.

Some people will argue that we just need better time management. Really, what we need is time awareness, paying attention to how we fill our days and what those choices are doing to our soul. Are our habits pulling us closer to Jesus? Are we using time to build relationships or just check off tasks?

God gave us time as a gift to live in, to be fully present so we can grow, rest, love, and reflect. Each moment is an invitation to say yes to what matters most. Maybe the question isn't, "How do I manage my time?" Maybe the more appropriate question is, "What kind of life am I invited to live and how does my time reflect that?" Because time is how we live. Time is how we become. Time is how we love.

Time as a Mirror

We might not often think of time as something we have a relationship with. Yet, we do. Just like we relate to people with trust or tension, joy or frustration, we relate to time the same way. Some of us feel like time is always slipping through our fingers. Others feel like we're constantly racing against it. Some try to fill every moment, so nothing is "wasted." Others numb out, wondering where the day went. We often speak about time with pressure in our voices: "I don't have enough time." "Where did the time go?" "I'm running out of time." "Time is getting away from me." When we live like time is always running out, we start living like we are running out.

What if time isn't our enemy? What if time truly is a holy gift? Maybe, instead of trying to "beat the clock" or "get ahead of time," we're being invited to enter into time differently – with gentleness and with awareness, perhaps even a little bit of grace. Time is where we experience love, where we notice beauty. It's where we learn to trust the slow work of God.

In our world today, many people see time as something to use up or fix. We try to squeeze every second, plan every hour, and keep time under control. Phone apps promise we can "master" our minutes. Quick tips and "life hacks" say they will help us "save" time. When our plans fall apart or our to-do lists get too long, we start acting like time is the enemy. We feel as if the clock is chasing us. It's no surprise that many of us feel what could be called time anxiety, that constant worry that there's never enough time. Our calendars are packed, and there's always something else waiting to be done. Our minds jump ahead to the next task while we're still in the middle of the current one. Underneath all the busyness, there's often a fear that if we don't keep up, we're not doing enough – and maybe we're not enough, either. This way of thinking about time is exhausting our calendars and our souls.

What if we stopped trying to squeeze more into our time and started making space within our time to breathe, to notice, to connect? What if we believed there is enough time to live well, love deeply, and follow Jesus at the pace of peace? Because the way we relate to time shapes the way we relate to life and to Jesus.

Jesus offers a completely different relationship with time.

In the Gospels, Jesus didn't just manage His time well, Jesus lived from a place of abiding – with God, with His mission, and with what mattered most. Every moment flowed from His identity and His commitment to God's kingdom. Jesus knew what He was called to do and, just as importantly, what He wasn't. He said yes to holy interruptions that aligned with love, and no to distractions that pulled Him off course. Jesus moved slowly enough to notice the woman reaching for His robe, to bless children others dismissed, to linger with friends, and to rest when the crowds still had needs.

He withdrew often, not because He was inefficient, but because Jesus knew that time spent with God shaped all the other moments. Even with the demands of teaching, healing, and leading, Jesus didn't rush. Jesus didn't let urgency define His days. Instead, He lived in rhythm with God, with the Spirit, and with the people right in front of Him. To follow Jesus, then, is to move the way Jesus moved: with margin, with intention, and with love as the compass. With time as sacred and holy ground.

If you really want to know what matters to someone, you don't have to ask – just glance at their calendar. Time is an honest storyteller. It may not reveal the story we hope to tell. It always shows the story we're actually living. Every appointment, every empty slot, every late-night email says something about our priorities. Our schedules highlight what we've shouted "yes" to, what we've ignored, and what we believe counts as important.

Sometimes that story looks beautiful: restful evenings, unhurried meals, time set aside for prayer, serving others, and simply being present. Those moments show our lives lining up with our deepest values like puzzle pieces fitting just right. Other times, the story looks scrambled: meetings stacked on meetings, no room for breath, constant scrolling instead of real connection. These aren't reasons to beat ourselves up, they are opportunities to pause, pay attention, and to ask different questions.

What am I saying "yes" to without thinking? Where am I crowding out what matters most? How could a small change open space for rest, prayer, or people I love? The way we use our time always tells the truth about what we trust, what we avoid, and what we believe matters. Time reveals what we trust. A tightly packed schedule might have little to do with productivity at all; it might point to a deeper reliance on control. When uncertainty feels uncomfortable, keeping busy becomes a way to manage the unknown. A full calendar can offer a sense of order, a way to avoid feeling vulnerable or out of control. Time also reveals what we avoid. Busyness can be a shield, a way to sidestep uncomfortable conversations, unresolved grief, or places within ourselves we're not yet ready to explore. When every moment is filled with activity, there's often little room left for hard truths and sacred invitations to rise.

Time reveals what we believe matters. Our calendars act like a map, tracing where our attention, energy, and presence are going. Each appointment, each commitment, each recurring task is like a marker on the journey of our lives. Are we investing in what actually nourishes our spirit? Or are we spending our days simply reacting, moving from task to task without ever pausing to ask what matters most?

Sacred time makes room for what's real. When we slow down, the quieter parts of our soul have a chance to speak. When we start to pay attention to where our time is going, we can begin to choose differently. We can start to invest in what actually reflects our faith, values and nourishes our soul. God meets us in the pauses, in the still, honest moments where truth can surface and healing can begin. Choosing to be present, even in silence, is an act of courage and grace.

More than Routine: Habits as Holy Invitations

Habits might seem like the most ordinary part of life. Brushing your teeth. Pouring the morning coffee. Checking your phone before your feet even hit the floor. Turning on the TV at the end of the day. These little actions live in the background of our days, mostly unnoticed and easily overlooked. Don't let their simplicity fool you. Habits are never just habits; they are not neutral. They are formative. Every habit points somewhere. Every habit carries a message about what matters to us – what we trust, what we long for, what we're avoiding, or what we're hoping to become. Habits are like tiny compasses, guiding how we move through the world. When you zoom out, you'll often find that your habits are shaping your relationship with yourself, with others, and with Jesus. Because behind every habit is something deeper. Beneath the habit is a belief. Behind the routine is a story. Every habit is formed by, and forming, your heart. The life you long for isn't created in a single decision; it's formed by the daily choices you repeat over time.

Sometimes our habits paint a beautiful picture. We pause to breathe, pray, or simply notice a sunset. On those days, the rhythm of our time feels intentional, almost like we're living from a clear purpose instead of a to-do list. Other times, the picture looks different. Our schedule fills itself instead of being shaped on purpose. The pace feels reactive, maybe even a scramble rather than a steady walk. And that's okay. That tension is part of being human. Every off-beat day is an invitation to return to holy rhythm, to choose one small practice that leads us back to what matters most. Grace meets us in both pictures, the lovely and the messy, always ready to help us start fresh.

Jesus knew this about the human heart: what we repeat shapes who we become. So, Jesus didn't just preach about love, rest, and trust, He practiced them. Over and over. The Gospels show Jesus' life rooted in rhythms. Jesus welcomed the dawn with prayer. While it was still dark, Jesus slipped away to speak with God. That daily conversation set the tone for everything that followed. He stepped away from crowds to rest. When demands grew heavy, Jesus withdrew to the hills or crossed the lake. Rest was part of faithful work itself. Jesus lingered at tables. Meals weren't rushed pit stops, they were sacred spaces for stories and healing. In shared bread and simple friendship, love came alive. Jesus traveled at walking speed. Moving from village to village on foot, Jesus allowed time for children to run up, for the sick to reach out, for lessons to unfold along dusty roads. No sprinting, no frantic multitasking, just a pace that left room for grace. These repeated choices formed the rhythm of Jesus' days and they reveal a pattern meant for us, too.

The very Spirit who guided Jesus guides you, too. Because of that, being faithful isn't about forcing your life to look like someone else's perfect schedule or strict routine. True faithfulness means paying attention to how Jesus is shaping you: your energy, your season of life, your unique gifts. It means letting the Spirit set your pace and show you the rhythms that help you love God and others. Instead of copying another person's formula, you're invited to listen for Jesus' personal, gentle direction and follow it with trust.

Running on Expectations

I once tried to become a morning runner. And by tried, I mean I gave it my full, type-A, perfection-leaning energy. I had a plan – a real one. Sneakers by the door? Check. Clothes laid out the night before? Check. Two alarms set? Naturally. (Because the first one was more of a psychological warm-up, basically a dare I always lost.) Every morning brought a new excuse dressed up in rationality: It's too cold. It's too hot. It's too dark. I have a slight headache – or maybe just a twinge? (Or is that self-sabotage wrapped tightly in these yoga pants?)

No matter how many checklists I made, the habit never stuck. Each time, I'd feel a little disappointed. Less because I didn't run, more because I had wrapped my worth, even my sense of spiritual discipline, into this one habit I couldn't make stick. What started as a desire for health and rhythm quickly twisted into another measuring stick I used against myself. Eventually, I had to ask, "Was running really what I needed in this season? Or was I chasing the image of the kind of person I thought I should be?"

Eventually, by grace, I began to see what was really happening. It wasn't that I lacked commitment (I had plenty of that). It wasn't even about motivation. I had motivation in the form of spreadsheets, alarms, motivational podcasts, and *Pinterest* boards full of "rise and grind" mantras. The problem was deeper than willpower. I was trying to force my life into someone else's rhythm.

I had picked up the belief that real discipline looked a certain way: waking before sunrise. Running before the rest of the world had their coffee. Journaling, meditating, protein shakes, green smoothies, inbox zero, and maybe a 5-minute plank just for fun (said no one ever!). Even though some of those practices were good and healthy, they weren't mine. They weren't rooted in my season of life, or the way Jesus was inviting me to live more deeply connected.

My body had a different message. No matter how many *Instagram* fitness gurus swore by 5 a.m. workouts and sunrise sweat sessions, my body wasn't having it. It didn't crave movement in the dark, pre-coffee hours. It didn't come alive just because the world said it was supposed to. My workout energy tends to arrive fashionably late. Mid-morning, early evening, that's when my mind starts to clear, my muscles feel ready, and say, Now. Now we can move. Health and holiness don't have a specific timestamp.

Once I stopped shaming myself for not thriving in the 5 a.m. club and started listening to my body instead, I gave myself permission to tune in – to notice when I actually felt most alive, not just when the world told me I should be. I began to ask gentler, wiser questions: When do I naturally feel most alert? When does my soul lean in rather than resist? When do I feel most open to move, to pray, to breathe, to reflect, not because I should, but because I want to?

It sounds so simple, doesn't it? It wasn't; at least not at first. Letting go of expectations I had absorbed from other people's routines and learning instead to notice when I actually had energy felt like a holy kind of rebellion. Honestly, it was liberating and freeing.

Instead of forcing myself into someone else's rhythm or chasing a version of life that looked good on paper but felt horrible in my body, I started doing something radical: I listened. I stopped trying to squeeze my soul into someone else's schedule and I started honoring my own. My God-given, Spirit-breathed rhythm. The one wired into me from the beginning, waiting patiently under all the noise and comparison and pressure. Do you know what I found? Energy I didn't have to chase or manufacture.

I used to cram in meditation during that groggy, half-awake hour known as o'dark-thirty, because it seemed like the "holy" hour. I've learned something much more holy: honesty. I've come to realize that my mind and heart don't open with the sunrise. They open about two hours into my day, around 7:30 or 7:45 a.m. That's when I can actually notice Jesus without my thoughts racing like I'm doing mental jumping jacks (rather than a cardio workout).

My creative rhythm doesn't clock in early either. I've heard plenty of stories about writers who get up religiously at 4:00 a.m., drink their cups of black coffee, and write feverishly into the middle parts of the afternoon with laser focus. That's not me. For me, creativity tiptoes in about two hours after my prayer time, somewhere around 9:30 a.m., and tends to linger through the early afternoon. (That might help explain why this manuscript took longer than expected.) I used to wonder if I was just undisciplined or missing some secret formula. I've learned to stop comparing and start paying attention.

When I begin the day with a walk, creativity often arrives even earlier. There's something about movement, about feeling my feet on the ground and letting my breath find a steady rhythm that clears space in my mind. But try to start something fresh later in the day? That's usually a lost cause. The words come slow, clunky, uncertain, and unclear trains of thought. When I revisit those late-day drafts, I can tell I was writing from fatigue instead of flow. I've learned, again and again, that I can't just push through, sit at my desk for 12 hours, and expect clarity to magically appear. Creative energy isn't something I can cue up on demand. It shows up when I stop forcing it and start paying attention to the rhythm God already placed in my day.

Some of my favorite moments come in the stretch of late afternoon or early evening, those rare times when the schedule thins out and there's room to breathe. I don't have to rush to the next thing or check another box, and there's space for a walk with our dog along a quiet path. Some days, when I enjoy an abundance of energy, that walk may naturally turn into a light jog. Only if my body says yes and only if it feels like an extension of joy rather than a demand.

These days, my evenings aren't about finishing one more thing or scrolling through everyone else's life. Instead, I choose connection. Sometimes it looks like a quick FaceTime with a friend I've been meaning to check in on. Other times, it's a slow walk with someone I care about. Sometimes it's as simple as sitting down for dinner with my family, giving each other the gift of undivided attention without our phones. When I carve out space for being truly present instead of producing, I feel more human. More whole. More aligned with what matters.

Reflection Questions: Running on Expectations

Whose expectations am I running on? Are they mine, someone else's, or ones I've absorbed over time without noticing? What have I believed I should do with my time? Where did that belief come from and is it still true for the life I long to live with Jesus? What do I feel pressured to prove and to whom? How is that pressure influencing my schedule, my energy, or my worth? Where in my calendar do I feel most misaligned? What parts of my weekly rhythm feel heavy, draining, or disconnected from who I am in Christ? If I were free from others' expectations, what would I choose differently? What small shift might I make this week that reflects that freedom?

Chapter 6
Holy Disruptions

WHEN I SERVED in the parish, I truly believed that a full calendar was a sign of faithfulness. The more packed the schedule, the more alive the ministry felt. If there were events every night of the week, meetings layered between worship planning and hospital visits, and a color-coded board that looked like a stained-glass mosaic of holy busyness, then, surely, I was doing something right. Surely, God was pleased. Right?

When Tired Becomes a Teacher

If I'm being completely honest here, there's a certain kind of rush that comes from being in demand. The rush of being the one people call, or the satisfaction of knowing your calendar is full because others trust you, or the false sense of pride that comes from feeling indispensable. If I really dig deep – beneath the ministry, the meetings, the endless to-do lists – there was something more going on underneath.

In ministry, it's easy for worth and value to get tangled up in numbers. Worship attendance. Volunteer sign-ups. How many people showed up, signed up, or gave. There's this unspoken pressure – sometimes internal, sometimes external – to prove that you're doing a good job by producing visible results. By growing something measurable. By showing that what you're doing is "working." And I fell for it.

If the sanctuary was full, I must be faithful. If the offering was strong, I must be effective. If the programs were packed, I must be doing God's will. Numbers rarely tell the whole story. They don't measure the quiet work of the Spirit. They don't capture the sacred conversations, the healing that happens off the spreadsheet, the faithfulness that no one sees.

Feeling the weight of financial pressure in the church, I tried to fix it. Every sermon felt like it had to be a home run. Every newsletter article had to be inspiring. Every program had to land just right. I over-thought everything. I over-analyzed every detail. I over-criticized myself when things didn't go perfectly.

There was one year I decided that our Vacation Bible School was going to be the event of the summer. I went all in. (Yes, believe it or not, VBS can be surprisingly competitive. Who knew ministry could feel like a marketing campaign?) I wanted ours to be the biggest, the brightest, the one people talked about long after it was over. So, we dreamed big. We brought in a real horse for the kids to ride. We blasted the publicity across town. Sure enough, the numbers soared. Parents talked. Kids showed up in droves. We became the VBS to go to.

Unfortunately, my heart wasn't in the right place. I was so focused on growing the numbers that I stopped noticing the souls. I was counting the sheep instead of feeding them. I had fallen into the trap of measuring ministry by attendance rather than transformation. Jesus doesn't see numbers or celebrate crowd sizes. Jesus sees people: each one with a name, a need, a story. The weary volunteer. The quiet child. The doubting parent.

In my drive to do more, I was missing the people right in front of me. I was missing the point. I had started to think of the program as mine: my vision, my success, my responsibility to grow. When it became mine, it stopped belonging to Jesus. When something that begins in service to Christ becomes centered on self, even with good intentions, it becomes disconnected from the Vine.

Exhaustion, it turned out, became my truth-teller. A holy messenger I hadn't invited yet desperately needed. Sometimes, it's only when we hit the wall, emotionally, physically, or spiritually, that we start paying attention to what our lives have been quietly trying to tell us. That's what happened to me during VBS, when the weight of "doing it all" finally caught up with me. My exhaustion was more than a sign of being busy, it was a signal. A messenger. A teacher. It pointed me to the habits I'd formed without realizing it. It spoke the truth I didn't want to face. That the things I was chasing weren't bearing the kind of fruit that abides on Jesus' Vine.

Most of us live by habits we didn't consciously choose. In this next section, we'll look honestly at a few of the most common habit traps that quietly wear us down.

Habit Trap #1: Stuck In Automatic Mode

Over-committing: yes becomes a burden. It often starts with good intentions. You want to help. You care deeply. You see a need and feel the pull to respond. You say yes because you can, because you've done it before, because it feels like the faithful thing to do. And then you say yes again. And again. Until your calendar is so full there's not a single breath of margin left.

Over-commitment often carries something more – an unspoken belief that your worth is measured by how much you do, how many people you help, or how well you hold everything together. When we say yes to everything, we often say no to the things that matter most. No to rest. No to silence. No to a few minutes of deep breathing. No to being truly present with the people and purposes that actually fill our souls. True faithfulness is about discernment, learning to say yes to what nurtures love: love of God, love of others, and love of self. Honoring the invitations that lead us deeper into our purpose, not just deeper into exhaustion.

If your evenings end with exhaustion instead of joy, if rest feels like a luxury rather than a rhythm, it might be time to pause and take an honest look at what's filling your life. Start small. Open your calendar and notice what's there. Which commitments feel energizing? Which ones drain you? Notice any patterns. Are your yeses coming from joy or from guilt? From a holy nudging or from fear of letting someone down? Try choosing one small "no" this week, something that doesn't align with your current priorities or season of life. Practice leaving space – on purpose. Protect an hour with no plans. Allow an unanswered email to wait. Give yourself permission to step out of autopilot and into intentionality. Your worth isn't found in how much you do. May you have the courage to choose what really matters. This is tender and vulnerable work.

Sometimes our over-commitment is less about time and more about identity. Maybe you grew up believing your value came from being helpful or agreeable. Maybe being needed gave you a sense of belonging. Maybe saying yes felt like love. Given enough time, those beliefs harden into habits. This is where self-examination becomes a holy invitation to heal. You might ask: What am I afraid will happen if I say no? Whose approval am I still chasing? What emotions or memories come up when I consider creating more space? These questions are doorways to deeper understanding. Sometimes the answers are layered and complex. This is where tools like journaling, spiritual direction, or working with a trauma-informed therapist or coach can create space for clarity and transformation.

If your schedule has been driven more by wounds, old stories, or patterns you never named, it makes sense that change takes time. Just like a branch can grow in a direction shaped by wind, weight, or lack of light, our lives often grow in response to forces we didn't choose, whether it's expectations we absorbed, roles we adopted, or pain we never named. Those patterns become familiar, even if they're not life-giving. We learn to keep saying yes to stay safe, to feel loved, to avoid conflict. We shape our schedules to survive. Survival is not the same as abiding.

Abiding begins with grace. Those old patterns didn't form overnight, and they won't disappear overnight either. They made sense in their season. They helped you cope, belong, protect your heart, or make it through. Now, they may be costing you more than they're giving and you've started to notice.

Abiding is a gentle reminder you were never meant to live disconnected from your Source. Even when your habits have been shaped by hurt, God is still tending to the soil. Still calling you by name. Still ready to grow something new in you.

In the vineyard, fruit doesn't appear the moment a branch connects to the vine. There's waiting. There's pruning. There's strengthening. Abiding is staying in that relationship long enough for the growing conditions to change. And they do change: with light, with care, with time. As you begin to notice what's been shaping you, you make room for new rhythms to take root. Rhythms that come from love instead of fear. You are being tended to by the true Vine. Even now, something sacred is growing.

Habit Trap #2: Distractions

It starts as a tiny tap. Just a quick glance at your phone, a harmless scroll, a little background noise to keep you company. In an anxious moment, that soft glow or ping feels like relief, a doorway out of boredom, loneliness, or stress. What begins as comfort can slowly become a pattern. Minutes expand into hours. The present moment slips through your fingers. You look up and wonder where the evening, or the year, went.

Psychologists call it a variable-reward loop. Each time you swipe, your brain releases a small pulse of dopamine, teaching you to keep reaching for the next hit of novelty or affirmation. Over time, those micro-rewards wire habits you hardly notice. What began as a tool now uses you, trading depth for distraction, connection for comparison, and rest for restless scanning. The mind grows jumpy, the body stays tense, and the soul forgets how to settle down. While scrolling is one of the most visible modern distractions, it's just one expression of a deeper pattern.

Not all distractions look like mindless scrolling. One of the most common modern distractions is digital overload. It's the constant loop of checking email and not because something urgent is waiting. Instead, it's because the act of refreshing gives a fleeting sense of control or progress. You tell yourself it will just take a second, but minutes, and eventually hours, slip by.

Then there's the background noise we've normalized: streaming shows or YouTube videos while folding laundry, answering texts, and half-listening to a podcast. It seems harmless, and maybe even efficient. With consistency, the constant low hum of input can keep the soul from ever finding silence. When every moment is filled with sound or screens, it becomes harder to tune into our inner life or to hear the Spirit.

Notifications only add to the noise. Every buzz, ping, and banner is a micro-disruption that fractures attention. The brain begins to live in a reactive state, jumping from app to app, message to message, with no real rest in between. This kind of task switching between browser tabs, devices, and platforms may look like staying on top of things, but it often keeps us from sinking into anything with depth.

Some distractions show up persistently in our minds. Even when your body is still, your brain may be running laps. You find yourself re-playing tasks you haven't finished, going over them like a checklist on repeat. Did I reply to that email? What was I supposed to pick up from the store? When will I find time to finish that project?

Then there are the conversations that haven't happened yet. The mental rehearsals of what you'll say, how someone might respond, and what you'll do if they don't understand. Trying to prepare for every possible future outcome can be subtle and exhausting, as your mind is constantly scanning for what could go wrong or what needs your attention next. These mental to-do lists become a soundtrack while you are sitting on the couch or lying in bed, which means you're not really resting. Your thoughts keep running ahead, dragging your nervous system with them. It becomes hard to experience the moment you're in because your energy is already spent on the moments that haven't arrived.

It can also be a sign that your mind is craving peace. The invitation isn't to shut your brain off (that's not how brains work). Instead, to notice when your thoughts are spiraling and gently come back. Naming what you're worried about, writing it down, or simply breathing with awareness can create just enough space for your mind to unwind. We can learn to be right where we are, even for a breath.

For some, being around others can become a way of avoiding ourselves. We might surround ourselves with conversation, activity, and even acts of service because we're quietly avoiding the stillness that might reveal what's really going on inside. We might focus on helping with someone else's pain because it's easier than facing our own. Emotional care-taking can become a shield, a way of staying busy with others so we don't have to pause and feel deeply. This kind of relational distraction is sneaky because it often looks like a connection. If you're wondering if this is showing up as a distraction, you might consider a gentle self-inquiry: When was the last time I was alone and truly at peace in that aloneness? What emotions come up when I'm not needed? What part of me is asking to be noticed? Whatever surfaces for you as you consider those questions, meet it with compassion. Remember, you are becoming more aware of the patterns shaping your days. If being alone feels unsettling, it may be a sign that part of you is longing to be heard. If you noticed grief, anxiety, or fear in the silence, it's a sacred invitation to tend to what's been buried beneath the noise. Wherever you are right now is a faithful place to begin. Simply notice what feels accessible in this moment. Maybe it's a slow breath. A few quiet steps outside. Start there. Small, honest practices are the ones most likely to grow.

Behavior-change theory reminds us that every habit follows a simple pattern: cue, action, reward. Our brains learn to associate certain moments with a need to check out, escape, or self-soothe. If we want to change our patterns, we start with noticing.

Begin with the cue. What's happening right before the urge hits? Is there a pause or slowdown in the conversation? A hard feeling rising up? A task that feels too big to face? A commercial? Often, it's not the distraction itself, it's the discomfort underneath it. Naming that moment with compassion creates space to choose something different.

Then, gently shift the action. When the scroll reflex kicks in, try placing your phone facedown and stepping outside for one breath of fresh air, allowing the light to find your face. Or lift your eyes and name three sounds around you. Run your hands under warm water. These small actions signal to your nervous system that you are safe, you are here.

Finally, consider the reward. Our devices offer quick hits of dopamine, while they rarely deliver real rest. Over time, encourage your body to relearn the slower rewards – shoulders softening or your breath deepening – a sense of grounding that says, This matters. This feels good, too.

Habit Trap #3: Work as Worth

This one is sneaky. It often comes in disguising itself as responsibility or ambition or even faithfulness. On the surface, it looks good – really good. Admirable, even. It might even be praised by others: Look how much she gets done! What would we do without him? You're rocking it. You're getting things done. You're showing up. You're making things happen. You're checking off the list. (Come on, tell me I'm not alone in this!) It feels like purpose. It feels like certainty. It feels like value. Until it doesn't. Until the checklist becomes a scoreboard.

What makes this trap so difficult to recognize is that it's socially rewarded. Psychologists call this performance-based identity, the belief that our worth is directly tied to our output. It's deeply rooted in many cultures and often reinforced by childhood experiences, work environments, or even the well-meant affirmations we've received ("You're such a hard worker!"). Over time, this belief becomes a habit: the constant drive to prove, to perform, to earn our place.

You've heard this before, but it bears repeating, especially in a world that keeps telling you otherwise: You are not what you produce. You are not your achievements. You are not your to-do list, your inbox, or your performance review. You are already loved. Your value is not up for negotiation. It doesn't fluctuate based on how productive you were today, how many people you helped, or how many goals you checked off. You are not a machine built to keep going without rest. You are not a project to fix or a problem to solve.

You are a person. A soul. A whole, living image of God.

There are no prerequisites for your worthiness. God did not create you for burnout. God created you for relationship. For rhythm. For love that flows from Jesus. If your heart has been carrying the lie that you are only as valuable as your latest success, let this truth interrupt it: Your worth is not on the line. It never was. You are already enough, because of who Jesus is.

Simplicity Changes Behavior

Complicated plans can feel exciting at first – color-coded charts, brand-new apps, and hour-by-hour schedules that promise a total life makeover. Yet, most of us know how those grand plans end: a week of determined effort, then a slow fade back to old rhythms. Why? Because willpower is a limited resource, and complicated systems require more of it than we can realistically give. The good news is that meaningful change doesn't depend on complexity; it depends on consistency.

You don't need to overhaul your life to experience real change. In fact, science and Scripture agree, transformation happens in the small things, repeated faithfully. Here's what we know from neuroscience and behavior research: habits are formed through a simple but powerful loop: Cue → Craving → Response → Reward

It starts with a cue, something you see, hear, feel, or anticipate. Maybe it's the buzz of your phone. The smell of coffee brewing. The pain of loneliness or stress after a long day. That cue stirs a craving (not just for the thing itself) for what it promises: connection, energy, escape, comfort, relief. So we respond, often without pausing. We open the app. We pour the coffee. We numb the ache with distraction or overwork or scrolling. When that response brings even a small reward – dopamine, a sense of control, a flash of relief – our brain logs it as useful. "That worked. Do it again." And it does. Again and again. Until that behavior moves to the background and becomes automatic, automating how we live, what we prioritize, and who we're becoming.

If a habit can be formed, it can also be reformed. Research on habit formation shows that behaviors stick when they are clear, easy, and satisfying. The simpler the action, the less friction you face. And the more likely you are to repeat it until it becomes second nature. Each small change you make is like a seed planted in faith. A vote cast for the kind of life you long to live. A shift toward a more rooted, present, Christ-centered way of being. It doesn't have to be big to be holy, it just has to be real and repeated.

Think of simplicity as clearing a path:
Clear the clutter.
> If your phone pulls you into endless scrolling, charge it in another room at night
> so bedtime belongs to rest instead of notifications.

Shrink the step.
> Instead of planning a 30-minute prayer session you rarely keep, start with one
> honest minute of quiet before breakfast.

Pair with a cue.
> Place your journal on the coffee maker. While the coffee brews, jot a single
> gratitude sentence. Tiny, automatic, done.

Celebrate the win.
> Each small success sends a positive signal to your brain: Yes, this matters. Let's do
it again.

Simple practices work like gentle rainfall on hard soil, softening the ground so
deeper change can take root. They respect your limits and honor your season of life,
all while nudging you toward healthier rhythms. As you consider the habit traps
we've explored – over-commitment, distraction, work as worth – ask yourself: What
is one simple next step I can take? Choose something so doable it almost feels silly.
Then repeat it tomorrow, and the day after that. Simplicity turns intention into reality,
one uncomplicated choice at a time.

One of the smallest changes I've made turned out to shift more than I expected:
Hydrating before caffeinating. Just one simple cup of warm water, first thing in the
morning. Before coffee. Before food. Before doing anything else.

At first, it didn't feel spiritual. Honestly, it felt like something a doctor or wellness
influencer might suggest. (Okay, it was something a wellness influencer suggested.)
Repeated every morning, this tiny ritual became more than a health tip. It became
a quiet act of intention. A way of saying, I will not rush. I will begin with what is
needed.

I used to reach for coffee before I was even fully awake. My feet would hit the
floor, and my hand would already be reaching for the mug. It was pre-programmed.
Literally. I'd set the coffee maker the night before to start brewing before my alarm
even went off. My caffeine lifeline was waiting for me before I even opened my
eyes. I told myself I needed it. That coffee was the only way I could function. Truth
be told, I was relying on a quick fix to carry my real exhaustion.

Now, I start with water. Just water. Some mornings with lemon. Always warm.
Always slow. I give my body a chance to wake up the way God designed it to.

That one small shift, water before anything else, has become a habit of alignment.
A micro-act of trust. A way of honoring how I was created. It's a reminder that I

don't have to start the day on fumes. I don't need to manufacture energy I haven't yet received. Before I check the news, open my inbox, or reach for anything external, I can let the simple things like water and breath remind me that I already have what I need to begin.

Small shifts add up. In fact, research and wisdom tell us that a 1% change might not feel like much in the moment. However, just this slight shift creates an entirely new outcome. A plane shifting its path by just one degree ends up hundreds of miles from its original destination. The same is true in our lives. One tiny turn, barely noticeable, can begin to carry us toward an entirely new direction.

Maybe that shift is how you start your morning. Maybe it's how you end your day. Maybe it's something as simple as where you set your phone while you eat dinner, or what you say to yourself when the to-do list goes unfinished.

Think about your day. Today, not some ideal version of tomorrow. What's one place where your habits feel misaligned with your deeper values? Now, what's one small change, just one percent, that could move you closer to the life you long to live? Maybe it's drinking a glass of water before the coffee. Or stepping outside for one minute of quiet before opening a screen. Or leaving one margin of time in your schedule where there used to be none. Whatever it is, let it be light, doable, and rooted in grace. That 1% shift might seem ordinary. In the hands of a God who multiplies loaves and fishes, and transforms water into wine, that one small act can lead to abundance you never imagined.

Spiritual Practices for Honoring Time
The "One Thing" Journal Prompt

Set a timer for 5 to 10 minutes to reflect: What is one small habit I want to try this week that aligns with who God is calling me to be? Write about what it could look like, how it might feel, and why it matters to you. Keep it simple, as a sacred conversation with yourself and Jesus.

Anointing Your Day

Each morning this week, take a drop of oil or water and place it on your forehead, heart, or hands. As you do, speak aloud: This day is a gift. I receive it with intention and grace. Allow it to serve as a physical reminder that time is something holy to inhabit.

One Percent Discernment Walk

Take a slow walk around your neighborhood, down a hallway, even in your back yard. As you walk, ask Jesus to show you one small shift (your one percent) that could help you live more fully aligned with your values and faith. Try not to force an answer. As you walk, just breathe and listen.

Start a "Holy Noticing" Log

Pick one day this week and jot down what you actually do, from morning to night. Nothing fancy. Just a few quick notes every few hours: What are you doing? How are you feeling? What's giving you energy? What's draining you dry? You may discover that your third cup of coffee isn't helping as much as you think. Or that a five-minute walk does more for your soul than an hour of multitasking. Or that you're holding your breath more than you realized.

Naming Your Automatic Habits

Step 1: Quiet Noticing

Find a quiet moment before bed, during your morning coffee, or even while washing dishes. Invite God into that space with a simple prayer: "Lord, show me what I do without thinking. Let me see my patterns through Your eyes."

Step 2: Trace Your Day

Walk back through your last 24 hours in your mind. What did you reach for first thing in the morning? How did you move through transitions? Between work and home, noise and quiet, people and solitude. Gently ask: What do I do without thinking? What happens automatically, again and again?

Step 3: List Without Judgment

On a piece of paper or in your journal, list 5 to 10 automatic habits, big or small. Be honest and be kind. Examples: Check my phone during pauses; Eat while distracted; Interrupt others without meaning to; Speak negatively to myself; Skip lunch but grab coffee.

Step 4: Prayer

Circle one habit on your list that feels out of alignment with your spirit or values. Trying not to fix it, just hold it in prayer: "Jesus, this habit has a story. Help me understand it. Give me the grace to release what no longer serves and the courage to choose something new in You."

Step 5: Blessing for the Journey

Placing your hand over your heart and breathing deeply, speak this aloud if you're able: "I am not what I repeat. I am who God says I am. And with every small awareness, I return to the One who is always making me new."

Listening to Your Body

Your body tells the truth, even when your mind tries to push through. It carries your stories, your stress, your joy, and your weariness. This practice creates space to listen with love, inviting Jesus into the physical experience of your day.

Step 1: Find a Safe Space to Pause

Sit or lie down somewhere comfortable, gently allowing your spine to lengthen and your shoulders to soften. If you feel safe doing so, close your eyes. Take three slow breaths, in through the nose, out through the mouth.

Step 2: Invite God's Presence
> Whisper a simple prayer, "Holy Spirit, I am here. Help me listen to the body You gave me."

Step 3: Gentle Body Scan
> Move your attention slowly from head to toe, speaking these words aloud or silently as you go:

"God, what are You showing me in my head?"
"What are You saying through my shoulders?"
"Is there peace or tension in my chest?"
"What do I carry in my belly?
"Are my legs heavy or restless?"
"What are my feet longing for? Stillness or movement?"
No need to change anything. Just notice.

Step 4: Let the Body Speak
> Where do you feel tired? Where do you feel strong? Ask, "What might my body be trying to say? What does it need from me today (i.e., nourishment, movement, rest, care, kindness)?"

Step 5: Closing Prayer of Blessing
> Place a hand over your heart or any part of your body that felt tender or in need of attention, praying, God of creation, You knit me together with care. Thank You for this body and the story it holds. Help me honor it, listen to it, and live in it with grace. Amen.

A Place to Begin
Anchored By The Saints

By now, you've started to notice how much of your life flows from habit. What's automatic, what's reactive, what's directing you beneath the surface. Maybe, as the fog of exhaustion begins to lift, you're feeling a deeper desire stir: You want to abide more deeply.

But how? When your thoughts race and your spirit feels frazzled, prayer can feel out of reach, like trying to tune into a faint signal through static. You want to connect with Jesus, but you don't know how to begin. That's why I want to introduce you to a resource that's become a companion on my own journey: *Kneeling with Giants* by Gary Neal Hansen. It's a wise guide into ancient rhythms of faith. Gary opened a door to the lived prayer practices of real people; people who, like you and me, were often tired, overwhelmed, longing for peace, and trying to find God in the middle of it all. He explained, "The prayers of the saints offer us a place to begin…a steady rhythm for our scattered hearts."

And oh, how we need that. As you begin reshaping your habits and reclaiming a sense of holy rhythm, you don't have to invent the path. You can walk the well-worn ones first. You can pray the words that held others. You can try on ancient practices until your own soul begins to find its footing. These Saints were followers. Abiders. Learners. Just like you.

If you're longing for something deeper, something rooted, time-tested, and soaked in grace, consider this next section your starting place. Let's meet a few of these companions. Let's borrow their prayers. Let's return to the One who's been waiting all along.

Martin Luther
Begin with What You Know

When Martin Luther was weary, he returned to what was solid, anchored in Christ, and familiar: the Lord's Prayer, the Ten Commandments, the Apostles' Creed. For Luther, prayer didn't need to be original, it needed to be real. He believed that prayer was a conversation between the child and the Creator, grounded in promise. He would take a single line, "Our Father who art in heaven" and let it slow him down and open his heart, allowing it to lead him into a deeper connection with God. If you've ever sat in silence, unsure of what to say, Luther offers this grace: You don't have to start with your own words. Allow Scripture to speak first and let the patterns of faith hold you until your own voice finds its way. Start where you are. Speak to God as you would a trusted friend.

St. Ignatius of Loyola
Review Your Day with God

St. Ignatius of Loyola offers a gentle practice to help you slow down and see clearly again. St. Ignatius believed that God is present in every part of our lives, not just in the obviously spiritual moments, but in our meals, our conversations, our work, our rest. To help us notice God's presence more deeply, he gave us the Examen, a simple, Spirit-led way to review the day with God. He taught us to ask simple questions: Where did I feel close to God today? When did I feel distant or distracted? What moments brought joy, laughter, or peace? What stirred sadness, frustration, or tension in me? What do I want to carry into tomorrow? What might I release or reframe with God's help? These questions help us notice God in places we might have missed. St. Ignatius teaches us that every day holds a thread of grace, and the Examen helps us trace it.

St. Teresa of Avila
Rest in God's Presence

While some saints guide us to speak, St. Teresa of Ávila gently invites us to listen. Her wisdom carries us inward to the quiet, sacred center of the soul where communion with God unfolds through stillness. St. Teresa taught that prayer is about awakening to the One who already dwells within. Deep within the heart of every person is what she called the Interior Castle, a sacred space where God lovingly waits with delight.

St. Benedict
Create a Life of Rhythm

In a world pulling us in every direction, St. Benedict offers us a rhythm that holds. St. Benedict, the father of Western monasticism, shaped his communities with a Rule of Life, a simple, structured guide for daily living that centered on balance, faithfulness, and intention. At the heart of it was this: ora et labora, pray and work, as a single rhythm. A way of living where prayer is not confined to the early morning or a church pew, but incorporated into every part of the day. For Benedict, peeling vegetables, sweeping floors, and studying Scripture could all become sacred acts, when offered with love. His rhythm was grounded in a way of anchoring the soul in God through the ordinary flow of life.

These saints – Luther, Ignatius, Teresa, Benedict – were not immune to exhaustion, distraction, or doubt. They lived in noisy, uncertain times and they wrestled with their humanity. Still, they chose to return, again and again, to the presence of God. They remind us that we don't have to have it all figured out. We don't have to pray perfectly. We simply need to begin.

Their prayers, their rhythms, their hard-won insights offer us something sturdy to hold onto when life feels scattered – as gentle companions, reminding us that faith is a relationship. One that can be tended moment by moment, breath by breath, habit by habit.

You don't walk this path alone. You are part of a living story. A holy lineage. A rhythm that stretches across centuries and into your very breath. Whether you're starting small, returning after a long pause, or simply longing for something deeper, trust this: You have guides. You have grace. Let's keep breathing. Let's keep abiding.

Start Where You Are

By now, you might feel a nudge: an invitation to shift something, to tend a habit, to make a little more space for the life you long to live. Maybe, right alongside that nudge is the familiar whisper of fear. What if I can't keep it up? What if I start and stop again? What if I'm just not disciplined enough?

You're not alone. Most of us have lived the cycle: a burst of motivation, a well thought-out plan, and perhaps even purchased a few new outfits for the occasion, only to watch it tank by Thursday. Life happens.

The dog throws up. The alarm doesn't go off. The toddler wakes up early. We miss a day, or five, and suddenly, shame shows up with its familiar script, See? You're just not good at this.

The purpose of a habit isn't to fix you, it's to form you. To open space where grace can breathe. To create room for the Spirit to move in ordinary, unnoticed moments. Before you rush ahead to change everything, pause. Take a deep breath. Let go of the pressure to get it all right. Let go of the belief that you have to do it all at once.

Begin right here. Exactly as you are. Not when your house is clean. Not when your calendar is clear. Now. Jesus is already here with a rhythm that holds you.

PART TWO

Becoming Whole

PART ONE OF our Breathing in Christ journey began with an invitation: slow down, breathe, and step out of the constant push to keep up. We started by noticing, without rushing to fix, what's already shaping you. What patterns are running your days? Which rhythms bring life, and which quietly drain it? Are your hours dictated by urgency and endless multitasking? Or have you begun to find pockets of stillness where Jesus feels near? This first stretch of our journey was the gentle work of turning your attention back to Love. We reframed the question from *"Am I doing enough?"* to "Who do I belong to?" Because your worth has never been in how fast you move or how much you get done; it is held secure in Christ alone.

And that, that alone, is holy work.

To breathe, really breathe – slowly and intentionally – in a culture built on instant response, is nothing short of sacred defiance. Every deep inhale is a quiet *no* to the lie that your value is measured by output, productivity, or speed. Each exhale releases the pressure to prove yourself. Your breath becomes a living prayer: *I belong to Jesus. I am not a machine. I am not a commodity. I am a beloved soul, Breathing in Christ.*

Maybe now, as you read this, you're beginning to see it more clearly. The rhythms that leave you weary, the habits that now feel noisy, the pressures that promise life but only hand you exhaustion. This is the middle of transformation. It doesn't happen all at once; it happens as you breathe, as you notice, as you stay present to Christ in the ordinary.

Breath is both biology and a holy invitation. A way back and a way forward. It's the doorway into presence and the rhythm of return. It won't fix everything. It will quietly lead you home to the center, where Jesus is already waiting. Every inhale becomes an open welcome, a *yes* to Christ who dwells in you, in your lungs, in this very moment. Every exhale carries grace: grace to release the weight you've been carrying, to let go of fear, pressure, and the tight grip of striving. While this slower rhythm might feel unfamiliar, it's actually your soul's first language. The pace you were made for. With each breath, you're more than taking in air, you are receiving Jesus and waking up to the Love that has always held you.

Now, we take the next step. We shift from simply breathing again to becoming whole. From slowing down to rooting our lives more fully in Christ. From catching our breath to discovering what it has been tethered to all along, a deeper source. A God-breathed identity spoken over you before the world ever gave you a name.

This next stretch of the journey is an invitation to trust – really trust – that life is a gift, and that you were always meant to live it in divine partnership. You are invited to move from the inside out, grounded in the holy promise: *You were made for this.*

Here, we begin to listen beneath the noise. Breathing becomes more than a pause. It becomes communion with Jesus. We start to return to wholeness. The questions shift. They no longer sound like calendar checks or performance reports. They start sounding like our soul:

Who am I, really – beneath the titles and roles? Who is Jesus, not only on Sunday mornings, but in the tension of bedtime routines and inbox overload? What stories have I been living from? Are they soaked in God's love or shaped by fear's demands?

Transformation rarely starts with all the answers. It begins with awareness. With curiosity. With letting Jesus step right into the middle of your layered story. He is already there in the ordinary, ready to help rewrite the narratives that no longer fit who you truly are.

That breath you've been holding for so long? You can let it out now. You are safe here. This is sacred ground. And you are not walking it alone.

This is the inner work, the sacred labor, of becoming whole. It's the quiet courage to let Christ walk with you into the hidden places: the wounds you've buried, the pieces you thought were too shattered to matter, the chapters of your life you've tried to forget.

Wholeness begins when you remember – really remember – your identity, your belonging, your origin. When the truth of who you are and *whose* you are rises to the surface, healing begins as you breathe again.

This work is tender. It is layered. It is beautiful. Every step you take toward Jesus is holy. Every breath that holds both truth and grace draws you closer to the One who never stopped calling your name. You were never lost to God. In Jesus' presence, every fragmented piece finds its place.

The way you move through life – your pace, your patterns, your choices – doesn't just happen. It comes from somewhere deep, shaped over time by story and survival, by love and by loss. These rhythms have roots. Roots that thread through memories you've tucked away, expectations you've carried without even noticing, roles you stepped into because someone once needed you to, and labels, spoken or unspoken, that tried to name you before you could speak for yourself.

That's why true transformation always starts beneath the surface. If we want to live lighter, freer, more whole, we first begin with curiosity. Not criticism. Not shame. Not the urge to overhaul everything at once. Just curiosity.

Some of what you carry is holy. True. God-spoken. You are seen. You are loved. You are held secure in Christ.

These truths were never meant to be earned. They were planted in the soil of grace long before you could strive for them. Meant to sink deep, to shape the way you live and move and breathe. They are worth remembering. Worth trusting. Worth letting reshape the way you move through the world.

Other voices have spoken into your life, too: some louder, some longer.

You have to earn your worth. Don't let anyone see you struggle. You're only as valuable as what you produce.

Maybe these messages helped you survive. They gave you structure when life felt chaotic. They kept you moving when standing still felt unsafe. Survival isn't the same as freedom. These messages never taught you how to rest. They didn't show you how to receive love without proving yourself.

Over time, they shaped the way you speak to God. Or they are the reasons you've stayed silent. They informed your relationship with desire, with risk, with vulnerability. They influenced how you give and receive attention, affection, even grace. They became the lens through which you saw yourself, the filter through which you interpreted the world – and maybe even the framework you imagined God using to measure you.

In Christ, you are invited to trade these wearying scripts for a truer story. A Love story where your value is in your belonging. *Whose* you are.

What was learned in survival can be unlearned in grace.

In Christ, you are no longer defined by your defense mechanisms. You are invited to live – fully, freely, deeply – in God's story, where love is not earned, where your name was spoken long before the pressure began.

You don't have to carry those old narratives forever. You're not obligated to keep living from a script someone else wrote for you. One drafted in fear, edited by rejection, and handed to you as if it were truth.

The striving can stop here.

In Christ, love, approval, and belonging are gifts already given. Grace speaks louder than the lies. Jesus invites you to lay down every distorted message, every heavy expectation, and trade them for holy truth.

This is sacred work. A rewriting at the soul level. It begins with two gentle but piercing questions:

What story am I living from? Is it even true?

These questions pull up roots. They shine light on what's been hidden. They give voice to what's been buried. As you name what's false, you create holy space for the true story to rise.

This is the journey of becoming whole. A homecoming to the self you've always been in Christ. Because your truest story has always been about being seen, known, and claimed by Love Himself.

The Apostle Paul understood something profound about becoming whole: sometimes, everything must come undone first.

Before encountering Jesus, Paul's life ran on a script fueled by perfectionism, performance, and approval. His worth was rooted in titles, achievements, and religious reputation. If identity were measured in accolades, Paul had it in abundance: elite training, influential connections, and an unstoppable intensity. From the outside, his life looked impressive. Inside, it was built on proving, striving, and control.

Then grace intervened.

On a dusty Damascus road, right in the middle of his momentum, Jesus showed up to ask for his heart. It was a full stop. A holy interruption. Jesus didn't shame Paul for the story he'd lived; He simply invited him to live a truer one.

This is the pattern of wholeness: the old scripts fall apart so God's story can rise.

Everything Paul once anchored his identity to – his résumé, his reputation, his religious perfection – came undone. In its place, Jesus offered something infinitely better: Himself. That moment was the beginning of Paul's wholeness. He released the life built on proving and received the truth of who he already was in Christ. Paul later wrote about it with breathtaking honesty:

I'm not saying that I have this all together, that I have it made. But I am well on my way, reaching out for Christ, who has so wondrously reached out for me. I've got my eye on the goal, where God is beckoning us onward to Jesus. I'm off and running, and I'm not turning back. (Philippians 3:12 -14)

Paul's transformation was a complete rewrite. He traded a life built on status, credentials, and religious achievement for something infinitely more sacred: a relationship with Jesus. All the striving, all the status, all the spiritual accolades – none of it mattered anymore. What mattered was Jesus. Paul no longer needed to build an identity; he began living into the one already given to him.

His story is living proof that it's never too late to live from a truer story, *God's* story. Even if you've spent years sprinting in the wrong direction. Even if you've chased the world's version of success or wrapped your worth in titles that no longer fit. Grace doesn't check your mileage. Jesus still shows up. He trades old scripts for new life. Turns spiritual exhaustion into sacred restoration. Takes worn-out résumés and rewrites them as redemption stories. This is what grace does: it interrupts, it redefines, it restores. The same Jesus who met Paul on the road still walks the roads you travel, ready to rewrite the story you've been living into the story you were made for.

Paul didn't just step away from his old life. He ran. One breathtaking encounter with the risen Christ turned everything upside down. The moment Jesus interrupted his story on the Damascus road, Paul stopped chasing status and started pursuing Someone far greater. From then on, his life became a wholehearted response to the grace that had found him first.

He ran in step with the Spirit, compelled by a love so powerful and so personal that he could say with unshakable conviction, "I'm off and running, and I'm not turning back." In Christ, Paul discovered what it meant to truly live; to release everything false and run full speed in the freedom of being loved. He had seen something in Jesus that made every other pursuit look like dust in comparison, and nothing else would ever satisfy again.

This is what becoming whole truly looks like. A daily movement toward the One who sees you, loves you unconditionally, and calls you by name. Wholeness begins when we let Jesus meet us on our own dusty roads. Walking with Jesus into wholeness means finding the gentle courage to release the stories that never fit, the voices that never spoke truth, and to receive instead the identity that has been waiting for us all along. When God's love comes first – always first – your tired soul can release the frantic striving and open to the fresh strength and life only Jesus can give. From that foundation, your values begin to shift, your intentions grow clearer, your habits take root in grace, and your choices align with the life you were created to live. Every step flows from the love that found you first.

Chapter 7
Made From Love For Love

TO UNDERSTAND THE heart of God, we begin with one of the most treasured words in all of Scripture: *hesed* (Hebrew: חֶסֶד). It's a word so full that no single English translation can contain it. Often rendered as loving kindness, steadfast love, mercy, or faithfulness, hesed is all of these – and more. It is the language of covenant, the heartbeat of grace.

Unlike fleeting human emotion, hesed is not just something God feels; it is what God chooses. It is a decision to remain. A mercy that moves. Love in action: loyal, fierce, sacrificial. It's the kind of love that stays when leaving would be easier, the kind that answers the soul's unspoken question: *Will you still be here when I feel like I'm not enough?*

Hesed Love

From the very beginning, hesed was the pulse of God's relationship with humanity. When Adam and Eve hid in shame, hesed came searching, covering their vulnerability and remaining nearby. It's the same love that found Hagar in the wilderness, went with Joseph into captivity, followed Israel through rebellion, held David in heartbreak, and ultimately put on flesh in Jesus – hesed incarnate.

Jesus laid down His life for all: for betrayers and mockers, for soldiers with hammers and thorns, for crowds that shouted "Crucify," and for hearts still wandering far from Him. While we were still sinners, hesed chose sacrifice. Covenant love wrapped itself in skin, stepped into suffering, and climbed onto a cross – not reluctantly, but willingly. Without blame. Without conditions. Hesed absorbs the cost.

And when Jesus breathed His last, this love did not end. Hesed doesn't expire. Three days later, love rolled the stone away. The grave couldn't hold back a love that keeps its promises. Death couldn't stop mercy from reaching us. This is hesed: unfailing love that endures, that acts, that remains – yesterday, today, and forever.

Then there's Jesus. The clearest picture of this upside-down Kingdom. He eats with sinners, touches lepers, honors tax collectors, and calls disciples with questionable pasts. His grace always goes first. On Easter morning, hesed called Mary by name outside the tomb, showed up on the Emmaus Road, and slipped through locked doors to speak peace to frightened friends. This is hesed: love that restores connection, steps into our confusion, and calls us back to hope. It is not only their story, it's yours too. The same love is calling you by name right now. Hesed shows up. And it stays. Always.

Called By Name

"But now, God's Message, the God who made you in the first place, Jacob, the One who got you started, Israel: Don't be afraid, I've redeemed you. I've called your name. You're mine." (Isaiah 43:1)

The world is loud. Notifications. Group chats. Emails marked urgent. Most of what comes at us isn't an invitation into connection; it's a demand for our attention. Every once in a while, someone says your name, not because they need something from you, but simply because they see you. Maybe it's the barista who remembers your order or the friend who texts just to check in, no agenda. There's something holy in that kind of recognition. It cuts through the noise and reminds you that you matter. That's what makes Isaiah 43:1 so breathtaking. Before God asked Israel to trust, follow, or obey, God made this crystal clear: "I have called you by name. You are mine."

I had a moment like this at a retreat a few years ago. It was a real retreat. No laundry piles calling my name, no dinner plans looming, no emails or dog hair waiting for me at home. Just quiet. Just space. Just a roomful of women, each of us wrapped in layers of what we couldn't quite leave behind.

The retreat leader started with a simple icebreaker: *Write who you are on a name tag. Whatever comes to mind.*

No further instructions. No prompts. Just me, a Sharpie, and the invitation to name myself.

It sounded easy – until I stood at the table holding my Sharpie like it might accuse me of something. My mind spun like a *Rolodex*, flipping through all the titles I've collected over the years: Deacon. Communications Director. Mission Coordinator. Mom. Ministry Leader. Each one told part of my story. Which one mattered most? Which one should I write?

I panicked and did what I've done so many times before: I reached for validation. I tried to squeeze three roles onto a few inches of adhesive paper, as if cramming my worth into that little rectangle would make it true. In that moment, I didn't want to be known, I wanted to be approved. I wanted to look capable, accomplished, enough.

A few minutes later, the retreat leader read from Isaiah 43. "I have called you by name. You are mine." Those words hit me like a spotlight. I realized I'd missed the point completely. If I had heard that verse first, I might have chosen differently. Instead of stacking titles like a résumé, I might have simply written: Beloved. Known. Jesus lover.

I saw what I'd been doing. Not just on that name tag but in my life. I was reaching first for the words the world had given me, not the words God had already spoken over me. I defaulted to my role-based identity. The capable planner, the decision-maker, the voice with the strong opinions (sometimes too many, I know). I started with effort, with the urge to impress, instead of starting with grace.

When we begin with Scripture, when God's voice becomes the starting point, everything shifts. God's Word forms us. It names us when the world tries to rename us. It tells us we are loved, chosen, and claimed before we ever accomplish or earn a thing. When you start from that place – belonging first – even small moments begin to change. You stop chasing identity in places that were never meant to name you. You start listening differently, showing up differently. That constant inner push to measure up begins to quiet.

You might find yourself saying "thank you" more often, letting it train your heart to notice how God is already present. You might turn off your phone for a few minutes just to sit in silence, letting Jesus remind you that you're already enough. You might say "no" to something and instead of feeling guilty, you feel free, because your value isn't tied to how busy you are.

Little by little, those choices become spiritual practices. Your everyday life becomes full of holy moments: washing dishes becomes gratitude, commuting becomes prayer, a quiet cup of coffee becomes communion with Christ.

I certainly didn't see it at the time, but that retreat moment was an invitation not just to rewrite my name tag, but to let God rewrite my story.

Before you ask yourself, *How am I doing? Where am I headed? Am I enough?* there's a quieter, deeper, more pertinent question waiting: *Whose am I?*

This naming comes first. Before you accomplish anything impressive, before you collect a single gold star, before you prove your faithfulness. Even before your biggest regret. Imagine Jesus standing right in the middle of your everyday life between the carpool run and the grocery aisle calling your name with love.

God always starts with relationship. Not performance. Not status. Not even spiritual maturity. This is Emmanuel, God with us, showing up in your commute when the traffic is heavy, in the coffee-stained journal where you're scribbling prayers, in the afternoons where you feel like you're barely holding it together.

Being called by name is hesed in action; God's loyal, pursuing love breaking into the ordinary and claiming you. The same Love that spoke Israel's name through Isaiah is still speaking yours. Steady. Faithful. Refusing to let go, even when you wander or forget who you are. This naming is restoration. It's God saying, "I see you. I claim you. I'm not going anywhere."

Because this Love calls you by name, you can trust that your life is anything but random. You were formed from Love, for Love. Deliberately, creatively, tenderly. If God went to the trouble to speak your name, you can be sure the rest of you wasn't left to chance. Every part of you has been thoughtfully shaped.

Spiritual Practice: Returning to The Name God Gives You

Your truest name isn't your Enneagram number, job title, or family role. It's not the version of yourself you post online or the mask you wear to get through the day. Those might be pieces of your story; however, they're not the whole story. You are called by hesed love. By name. Take a few moments to reflect:

What names have you been living from lately? Not just the ones others use, but the ones you say to yourself when no one else is listening. "Busy." "Barely Holding It Together." "Not Enough." "Imposter." Are those names really true, or are they scripts from a past season that you've outgrown?

Are there old roles you've been performing that no longer serve you? Overachiever? People-Pleaser? The One Who Has It All Together? What would it look like to set them down gently, with gratitude, and make space for who you are becoming?

Which names feel rooted in love, in truth, in Christ? "Beloved." "Chosen." "Enough." "Held." Think of the moments when you feel most grounded and safe, when you sense you are fully seen and known. Where are you? Who are you with? What are you doing?

How might life change if you lived from those names more often? Would you breathe easier? Let yourself rest? Say yes and no with more freedom? Stop hustling to earn what's already been given?

Choose one name you long to live from this week. Write it down. Place it where you can see it often so it becomes a prayer: *This is who I am. This is Whose I am.*

A Simple Breath Prayer: Remembering Whose You Are

When the noise gets loud – when old labels like *Not Enough* or *Unworthy* start to rise – pause. Right where you are. And breathe this breath prayer:

Inhale: *You call me Beloved.*

Exhale: *Help me live from Your name.*

Repeat until your breathing slows and your heart settles. Allow the words to drop from your head to your heart. Write your chosen word (Beloved, Chosen, Enough, Held) where you'll see it throughout the day: on a sticky note by your desk, traced on your bathroom mirror, as your phone lock screen, on your dashboard.

And I mean it – write it down. If you don't put it somewhere you'll see it, chances are you'll forget as soon as the noise of the day starts up again. Keep it front and center – on your mirror, your fridge, your planner – anywhere that can catch your eye and remind you of the truth. Invite it to interrupt your day and call you back to who you really are.

Chapter 8
Let It Be – Trusting God in the In-Between

LIVING FROM THE name God gives you is beautiful and sometimes scary. It's one thing to know you are beloved. It's another to trust that name enough to live like it's true. That's why I love Mary's story. She shows us what it looks like to pause, listen, and respond to God even when the timing feels impossible and the calling feels bigger than you.

Mary was a young woman from an out-of-the-way town called Nazareth. No résumé. No title. No platform. No spotlight. Just a heart open enough to receive what she never saw coming. Luke 1 tells us she was going about her day. Maybe sweeping the floor, maybe kneading bread, maybe just waiting for the pita to rise – when eternity interrupted her ordinary life. An angel appeared out of nowhere, "Greetings, favored one. The Lord is with you" (Luke 1:28).

Now, I don't know about you, but if an angel just dropped into my kitchen unannounced while I was still in my pajamas and before I brushed my teeth, I'd probably spill my coffee and apologize for the mess. Mary, on the other hand, doesn't faint. She doesn't scramble to make things look perfect. She pauses. She listens. She lets the moment breathe.

What unsettles her isn't the angel; it's the greeting. *Favored one.* This is more than a polite introduction or a heavenly compliment. This is covenant language. It's hesed love naming her, claiming her. I get why she's startled. *Favored? Me? Are you sure you've got the right kitchen?*

We still ask that, don't we? Not just about angels showing up, but about the idea that we could really be loved, chosen, and called by God, especially when we feel wildly unqualified, painfully ordinary, or like the timing couldn't be worse.

Mary doesn't pretend to understand. She doesn't scramble for certainty or try to control the outcome. She simply stays in the conversation with God, hands open, heart available. This is where faith begins. With the courage to lean in closer when everything feels uncertain.

Mary's *yes* came before Bethlehem, before the manger, before the journey began – because she was already known, already favored, already held by God's hesed love. Her *yes* wasn't about proving herself worthy; it was the natural response of someone who trusted that God's word over her life was true.

This is what trust in Jesus really looks like: holding space for mystery without forcing it to make sense right away. It's choosing to believe – even if just by a thread – that God's word over your life is louder than your inner critic and stronger than your limitations. Sometimes the bravest thing you can do is simply stay in the conversation with God. To acknowledge, *I don't get it, Lord, and I'm still here. I don't understand. I'm listening. I don't feel capable. If You say I am, then let it be.*

Trust doesn't mean you've figured everything out; it means you've chosen to remain. To stay in the tension, in the waiting, in the wondering and let God stay with you there. Fear might still have a voice. It doesn't get the final word. Grace does.

When you find yourself in that hallway between what was and what's not yet – between the door that just closed and the one not yet open – you don't have to run. You don't have to force the next thing. You can stand still. You can breathe. You can plant your feet in the soil of hesed: the unshakable promise that God is with you, Jesus is for you, and the Holy Spirit will never leave.

Mary knew something about that hallway space – that holy in-between where everything feels suspended. Her whole life shifted between the angel's announcement and her next step. She didn't demand a blueprint or a guarantee. She simply opened her heart to God's promise and said, "Let it be with me according to your word."

Those nine words rewrote her story and changed the world.

The same God who called Mary favored calls you beloved. That promise is strong enough to live from. Not just on your best days, but in the middle of the laundry piles, the hard conversations you'd rather avoid, the disappointments that hurt and the moments of joy that catch you by surprise.

Maybe you've felt small or uncertain. Maybe you've wondered if you're really ready for what's ahead – or if Jesus might have knocked on the wrong door. Maybe you've offered up your own quiet "let it be" in the dark, not sure if anyone was listening. Mary's story reminds us that God's promises don't rest on your qualifications, your confidence, or your perfect clarity. They rest entirely on God's love. A love that has already named you, already chosen you, already gone ahead of you.

That love is here, right now, as you take the next step through whatever today holds.

Creation in the Ordinary

Mary's *yes* didn't stay in Nazareth. It moved with her – through morning sickness and midnight worries, through conversations with Joseph, through the long road to Bethlehem, through swaddling cloths and sleepless nights. Her *yes* became embodied, ordinary, lived.

That's the invitation for us too. Saying yes to God is more than the next fleeting moment. It's a way of being.

Love is the framework of our lives. A love with breath, intention, and a steady pulse. When God breathed life into humanity, it wasn't with a casual, "Good luck out there." It was personal. Purposeful. Breath-on-skin intimate. Soul-to-soul intentional. "Let us make humans in our image" (Genesis 1:26). That moment was the beginning of God's invitation to experience life in the Spirit. To be made in God's image means you are wired to reflect holy beauty. You are more than a spectator in the story of redemption. You are a participant. A bearer of light in the ordinary moments of your day.

You are made to nurture, to co-create, to speak life into tired places, to hold space for grace in conversations, coffee shops, and car rides. This is the rhythm you were made for. Not exhaustion. Not perfectionism. Not endless performance. Love. The kind shaped by Jesus, carried by the Spirit, rooted in joy. That's why it feels so good to bring something into being.

When you make dinner and someone smiles, "Wow, this is great!" When you sing like no one's listening (even if they are). When you clear a cluttered counter and breathe easier. When you tape a child's drawing to the fridge like it's a masterpiece. When you repair something instead of tossing it away. When you plant flowers and wait for color to break through the soil. Each moment is a reminder: creation is still happening. And you get to join in.

Think about bread. Kneading dough, waiting for it to rise, pulling it warm from the oven. You are entering the same creative rhythm that first shaped you from earth and breath. In your hands, flour and water rise into something more; a shared work with the One who gives the seed, the rain, and the life that sustains it all.

Or painting. Brush meeting canvas, color spilling into light. From blankness to beauty, you mirror God's "Let there be light" moment as nothing becomes something.

Or writing. A few lines of encouragement in a card or text. Hope moves from your heart through your hand into theirs. You remind a weary soul that love still shows up in envelopes, on sticky notes, in text messages.

Even your table can become holy ground. Whether it's candlelight and homemade bread or takeout on paper plates, gathering people together mirrors the welcome of Jesus. He turned meals into sanctuaries. He made space where belonging could meet brokenness.

Jesus is not absent from ordinary places. He's in your baking, your budgeting, your boundary-setting. In your choice to respond with kindness instead of cynicism. In that deep breath you take before answering. In the moment you keep showing up, even when your heart wants to shut down.

This is what it means to live from your divine design, bearing the image of God in the Tuesday afternoons and grocery store lines and bedtime routines.

You are a living, breathing extension of the One who makes all things new. Every day is an invitation to co-create with God: to bring life where there is emptiness, light where there is darkness, and grace where there is brokenness. This is what you were made for: love rooted deep and growing in ordinary soil. This is holy ground. And you are already walking in it.

Grace Meets the Gap

Even after we've said our own yes to God, after we've remembered we are named and loved, we still wake up some mornings feeling like we must earn it all over again. (Ask me how I know.)

You can know that grace is a gift, no strings attached – and still carry a low dose of anxiety asking if you've done enough, been enough, held it all together well enough. (Trust me, I've been there, too). It's strange, isn't it? How we can know something is true and still live like it's not? Knowing Jesus loves you and actually living like you're loved – those are two very different muscles. One is belief. The other is practice. And practice takes time. It takes rewiring old patterns. It takes patience. It takes grace. More than we think we need, and more than we often know how to receive.

There's a gap between what we know in our heads and what we trust in our hearts. Sometimes that gap feels like a desert: dry, empty, uncomfortable. Sometimes it feels like failure. That gap is exactly where Jesus does his best work and is precisely where he keeps showing up. Meeting us again and again in the middle of the tension, the middle of the mess, the middle of the not-yet.

We all carry gaps. Places where our words say "grace," but our calendars say "earn it." Places where our theology says "beloved," but our habits scream "prove it." Places where we know we're not alone and still wake up bracing to carry the day ourselves.

Naming the gap is a spiritual opening. It's where formation begins. When we name the gap, we stop pretending. We stop performing. We begin to make space for Jesus to meet us as we really are.

Remember the season when my head knew I was God's beloved, but my calendar double-booked folks? I said *yes* to everything – every request, every need, every good cause because deep down I feared that saying no might make me look selfish or lazy. My belief said grace is enough, but my habits said prove it.

That gap wasn't something I fixed overnight. It was something I noticed first. Noticing became the start of healing. Each time I caught myself saying *yes* out of fear instead of freedom, I would pause and pray, "Jesus, meet me here. Show me what love looks like in this moment." Little by little, grace began to reshape the way I made decisions.

Your gaps will look different from mine. They're there to invite you closer to the One who already knows them. Take a moment to consider:

> Where do you feel the tension between what you believe and how you live?
>
> Are there places where you know you are forgiven and still find yourself carrying guilt?
>
> Are there relationships where you believe in grace and still hesitate to offer love freely?
>
> Are there habits where you believe in God's rest and still find yourself striving to keep up?

These questions are here to uncover the places where God's Spirit is still at work, tenderly forming you from the inside out. The gap is where grace is still unfolding. Think of it as holy ground, a space where Jesus kneels beside you and says, "Let's walk this together." Every time you notice the tension between what you believe and how you live, you're noticing the very place God wants to bring healing and freedom. This noticing is itself an act of faith. It's the first step toward transformation.

You don't have to close the gap on your own. The Spirit is already at work, slowly rewiring your patterns, reshaping your desires, and teaching your heart to trust what your head already knows. Grace does the heavy lifting. Your part is to stay open, to stay honest, to keep naming the places where you need Jesus.

This is a good place to stop and breathe. Sit quietly for a moment and notice where you feel the tension between belief and behavior. As you hold those places before God, pray these words with me and trust that Jesus is already near.

Let us pray. Lord, here is the space where I struggle. Here is where my heart lags behind my faith. Step into this gap with Your grace. Teach me to rest in Your kindness instead of rushing to prove myself. Thank You for meeting me with compassion, never disappointment, and that You will finish what You've started in me. Amen.

Chapter 9
Naming Your Sources of Exhaustion

WE'VE SPENT THE last chapters breathing in the truth that you are named, known, and loved by God. You can trust Jesus with your yes, even when you don't have the whole blueprint.

But what happens when you know all that – and you're still tired?

Not just a little sleepy. Not just "I could use another cup of coffee" tired. I'm talking about the kind of exhaustion a good night's rest won't fix.

We often feel it before we ever find words for it. At first, it was just a little harder to get out of bed. A little more effort to smile when someone asked how you were. A little less energy to care about the things that used to matter.

And now – it's everywhere.

In your breath.

In your body.

In your bones.

You're exhausted.

Maybe you haven't had the words for it or the space to say them out loud. Here, in this space, you don't have to pretend. You don't have to say, "I'm fine," when you're not. You don't have to feel guilty for being worn down or explain why you're tired or justify why your soul feels empty.

You get to be honest.

Let's be clear about something: Jesus never asked you to run on empty. He never expected you to keep pouring out when your soul is dry. The drive to prove and to perform was never Jesus' invitation. In fact, Jesus offers something completely different.

He came precisely because He knew this is how we'd feel sometimes. He knows the weight you carry. Even the pieces you've hidden from everyone else. He knows the pressure that wakes you up at 2:00 a.m. and the expectations that feel impossible to meet. *Jesus isn't asking for more from you. He is offering more of Himself to you.*

On the cross, He said three words that changed everything: "It is finished." (John 19:30). When Jesus spoke those words, He was speaking freedom over every soul trapped in the exhausting cycle of proving and performing. Jesus' final words were a declaration of rest. A promise that the cycle of running on empty was over. He died so you could stop running on fumes in the here and now. He died so you could breathe again. Those three words were a holy exhale over all of us who feel like we can't keep up.

It is finished.

The guilt that keeps you second-guessing your worth. The pressure to be perfect, to never let anyone down. The need to hold it all together. Because maybe the pace you've been keeping has become so normal you've stopped asking if it's even optional. (It is). There is another way – and Jesus is already inviting you into it. These words aren't just about what happened on a hill two thousand years ago. They are for us right here, right now. Jesus invites you to breathe again. Right where you are. To stop gasping for air under the weight of expectations and simply inhale grace.

To breathe again, we first notice what's making it so hard to catch our breath. We name what's pressing on our chest, what's draining our energy, what's keeping us running on fumes. Because when we notice, when we name it, we open space for Jesus to meet us there – with compassion, with gentleness, with rest.

It's an act of courage to say:

This is where I'm tired.

This is where I'm stretched too thin.

This is where I'm carrying more than I was meant to hold.

This chapter will help you name what drains you while inviting Jesus to bring life to what feels broken. By the time we're finished, you'll be taking small, grace-filled steps to live from Jesus' love in real, tangible ways. *Jesus Knows This Kind of Tired*

One of the things I love most about Jesus is that He knows what it means to be tired. The *I-need-to-step-away-because-it's-all-too-much-right-now* kind of tired.

Jesus didn't float above the mess of human exhaustion.

He entered it.

Jesus lived it.

He honored it.

Scripture doesn't hide this from us. In fact, it shows us again and again a Savior who doesn't merely understand tiredness in theory, but who felt it in His body, just like we do.

When the woman in Luke 8 reached out to touch the hem of His robe, Jesus didn't just keep moving. The crowd was pressing in on all sides. The urgency of need was everywhere. Jesus could have kept going. Instead, Jesus stopped. He felt the drain of power leave Him, and He named it: "I noticed that power had gone out from me." (Luke 8:46).

Even Jesus knew what it felt like to be poured out. To feel something drain from Him, to sense the cost of healing, of giving, of being present. He didn't brush it off. He noticed. He honored it. This moment matters because it reminds us that even the Son of God did not ignore what it cost to pour Himself out. He paid attention to His own depletion, and so should we.

After feeding the five thousand, a miracle that still leaves us awestruck, Jesus didn't linger to soak in the applause or sign autographs on loaves of bread. Jesus withdrew (Matthew 14:22–23). He stepped away from the crowd, the need, the noise. He went up on the mountain to pray, to breathe, to rest. There was no rush to the next event, no pressure to do more, be more, prove more. Jesus honored His own need for stillness, for solitude, for connection with God. There was no shame in stepping away, only wisdom. This is holy rhythm. Jesus models something most of us were never taught – it is okay to notice when you've given all you can. It is okay to say, "That took something out of me." It is okay to step away.

Even Jesus stopped.

When the disciples returned from their own ministry, adrenaline pumping, Jesus didn't meet them with a clipboard and a fresh to-do list. Jesus saw them. Jesus saw what pouring out had cost them. He acknowledged their limits and said, "Come away with me and rest a while." (Mark 6:31). He invited them to rest, as if rest was as holy as the work itself. As if stopping was as sacred as starting.

Jesus teaches us that rest isn't what you squeeze in after everything else is done. It is part of life. It is part of the rhythm of faith. It's what roots us again in who we are and who God is.

And then there's Gethsemane.

The garden.

The edge of the cross.

The weight of the world pressing down.

Jesus doesn't pretend He's fine.

He weeps.

He prays.

He tells the truth.

"My soul is deeply grieved, even to death" (Matthew 26:38).

That is raw honesty right there. That's Jesus saying, "I'm at the end of myself." That's Jesus modeling what it looks like to speak limits out loud.

If Jesus, fully divine, fully human, took time to step away.

If Jesus paused after pouring Himself out.

If Jesus made space to breathe, to grieve, to rest, to be alone with God.

Why do we imagine we're the exception? Why do we carry the silent expectation that we should be able to do it all, without pause, without margin, without need? Why do we believe that holding everything together is the mark of faithfulness, when Jesus Himself let go, stepped back, and let God hold Him? This is wisdom. This is holy invitation.

Your worth was never meant to be measured by your productivity. Your belovedness is not proven by your stamina. Your identity in Christ is not about pretending you're not tired when you are. If Jesus made space to rest, to name His weariness, and to let God meet Him there, you can too.

An Invitation to Get Honest

Not all exhaustion is the same. Some of it lives in your body. Some of it lingers in your spirit. Some of it seeps into your emotions or relationships or the space between breaths. Some of it comes from doing too much. And some of it comes from holding too much grief that's never been spoken aloud, expectations that went unmet, stories you've never felt safe enough to tell, old patterns that play on repeat, draining your energy every time.

The world doesn't give us much language for this kind of weariness. We know how to say "busy". We know how to name stress. We can laugh off burnout like it's just part of modern life.

But soul-weariness? The exhaustion that steals your joy, your peace, your sense of purpose. We rarely make space for that. Instead, we're told to push through. To try harder. To drink more caffeine. To keep going, no matter the cost.

You know what's missing from that script?

Jesus.

Compassion.

Permission.

Grace.

When Jesus walked the dusty roads of Galilee, He saw people just like you and me. People carrying invisible weights. People running on empty. And what does Jesus say to them – to us? *"Come to me, all you who are weary and are carrying heavy burdens, and I will give you rest."* (Matthew 11:28).

Come. Come weary. Come worn. Come right in the middle of the mess you don't know how to clean up. Come with the questions you don't know how to ask and the answers you're too tired to look for. Just come. Right now. Exactly as you are.

The world will tell you strength means never slowing down. Jesus says real strength begins when you stop long enough to let Him hold what you can't.

One script leaves you empty. *Only one will breathe life back into your soul.*

The Many Faces of Exhaustion

Exhaustion isn't always loud. It doesn't always announce itself with flashing lights and blaring sirens. Sometimes it shows up like a slow leak. Barely noticeable at first. Quiet. Persistent. Draining. It's kind of like that dripping faucet you keep meaning to fix. At first, you barely notice it. Just a drop here. A drop there. You tell yourself, "I'll get to it eventually."

Days turn into weeks and, slowly, it accumulates. A little less patience here. A little more frustration there. You brush it off, *I'm just busy. It's just a season.* Inevitably, the season stretches longer than you planned. You promise yourself it'll slow down soon. Spoiler alert: it doesn't. The leak keeps dripping.

Then there are other times when it's not a slow drip, it's a full-on, tidal-wave, *where's-my-life jacket* kind of overwhelm. It's the morning. Your feet hit the floor and you already want to climb back into bed. It's when you're sitting in traffic, gripping the steering wheel, and you realize you've been holding your breath so long, you could probably make the Olympic swim team.

Sometimes, it's triggered by something small: a smart comment, a spilled coffee, a forgotten appointment. Sometimes, it's nothing at all. Just a wave of *too much* that breaks into an ordinary Monday afternoon.

You try to catch your breath. You hold back tears. You shake it off because there are things to do, people to take care of, expectations to meet. Shaking it off isn't enough because *exhaustion always leaves a trail.*

Exhaustion isn't invisible. It marks its territory.

Sometimes it looks like dark circles under your eyes, proof that you've been fighting battles even in your sleep. Sometimes it looks like a stack of unopened mail that's now doubling as a coffee table. Sometimes it's the feeling of dread in your stomach when you look at your calendar. Sometimes it's the way your shoulders stay hunched even when you're trying to relax, as if your body is saying, *Relax? I don't even know her.*

It might look like:

Impatience. Snapping at the ones you love because you can't quite put your finger on what's wrong, but everything feels like too much.

Forgetfulness. Walking into a room with purpose, and then just standing there. (You look around as if the walls might remind you why you came in. They never do.)

Numbness. Not feeling much of anything anymore because it's all just *too much.* Even the things you used to love feel like tasks.

You know that drawer in your kitchen that just collects stuff? Like you don't even remember putting half of it in there, yet, somehow, it's jam-packed with expired coupons, three batteries of questionable power, and a screwdriver that may or may not belong to your neighbor? *That's what exhaustion is like.* It piles up, quietly and persistently, until you can barely shut the drawer. Then one day, you go to grab a pen, and the whole thing jams.

Exhaustion always leaves a trail, even if you're the only one who sees it. *That trail can lead you back to healing.* It's an invitation to trace your steps, to see where the leaks are happening, to notice where the waves keep crashing. Jesus doesn't just see the trail; He meets you in it. He walks it with you, inviting you to pause, to rest, to come to Him and breathe.

There's no catch. No asterisk. No fine print. Just an invitation.

To step off the hamster wheel.

To drop the weight you've been carrying.

To breathe a little deeper.

To rest – a real rest – that doesn't require you to earn it first.

Jesus invites you to understand why you're so tired in the first place. Real rest is more than sinking into the couch at the end of the day. It happens when you let go of what's been wearing you down from the inside out.

Here's where we go even deeper. You know that saying, "You can't heal what you won't name?" There's a reason for that. You can't fix a leaky pipe if you don't know where the drip is coming from.

And exhaustion? It's the same. To move toward the kind of rest Jesus promises, we stop and assess where our energy is leaking. Exhaustion leaves clues; patterns, habits,moments we've ignored. We trace the trail that exhaustion has left behind. When we understand the source of our fatigue, we can meet it with compassion. We can choose differently. In that choosing, healing begins.

Before we take another step, let's pause. I prayerfully invite you to be honest with yourself. This is sacred ground. You are safe here. If you're tired, say so. If your heart is heavy, let it speak. If you're carrying more than you should, invite Jesus to help you lay it down. Begin right here, right now, just as you are. Jesus is here. I'm here. We're holding space for you to exhale.

In the pages ahead, we'll explore the most common sources of exhaustion. These are the everyday burdens that pile up. The most common culprits of slow leaks that drain your energy, deplete your spirit, and leave you running on empty. Some of them will sound familiar. Some might surprise you. All of them matter because every leak, no matter how small, affects the whole. As we talk through them together, I invite you to stay open, stay curious, and stay kind to yourself. As we bring each source into the light, my prayer is that you will find the courage to name it, the grace to release it, and the joy of breathing freely again.

Physical Exhaustion

Did you know that in Japan, there's actually a word for dying from overwork? *Karōshi.* It's such a common issue that they've had to name it. In one of the most advanced societies in the world, people are literally working themselves to death. Actually collapsing from sheer exhaustion. While that might seem extreme, I wonder if American culture is really all that different. While we may not have an official word for it, we've normalized pushing past our limits and treating rest as a privilege instead of a priority.

Here's the heart of the matter: your body is talking to you. All the time. Every ache, every yawn, every ounce of anxiety is your body waving tiny flags, trying to get your attention. It's not just *in your head*. Your body is carrying your experiences with you. Dr. Bessel van der Kolk, in his ground-breaking book *The Body Keeps the Score*, explains how our bodies are living, breathing archives. They store experiences, not just the good ones, but the hard ones. The exhausting ones. Your body doesn't just experience stress, it *remembers* it.

Your body is talking to you. It's saying, *I'm holding onto something here. Can we talk about it?*

Dr. van der Kolk's research reveals that trauma and chronic stress don't just pass through us, they *live* in us. Our bodies become filing cabinets for experiences that were too heavy to process in the moment. If you've ever flinched when someone raised their voice, even though they weren't yelling at you, your body was remembering. If you've ever felt your heart race when you smelled a familiar scent that brought you back to a difficult season, your body was remembering.

Van der Kolk calls this "somatic memory," the way our muscles, tissues, and nervous system hold onto things long after our conscious minds have moved on. Your body can actually *react* as if it's still living in that moment. Your heart races. Your palms sweat. Your shoulders tense. Your body is remembering, *Hey, I've been here before.* It's also why you might be rubbing your neck right now and wondering why it feels like you're carrying a backpack full of bricks.

Your muscles are messengers, an alerting system. They don't necessarily ask if the fire is big or small, they just know there's smoke and scream for your attention. The difference is, with your body, it's not just fire. It's stress, tension, hurt, and unspoken words. When we don't address these feelings, our body doesn't just shrug and move on. It stores them. It builds up tension until we finally listen – or until it has to shout.

Headaches. Tight shoulders. Clenched jaw. It's our body's way of saying, *There's something here. Pay attention.*

The irony? Most of us have trained ourselves to ignore it. We pop some ibuprofen, pour another cup of caffeine, and push through like nothing's wrong. We get so practiced at faking "fine" that we hardly hear our bodies begging us to slow down. This is what I love about Jesus. He *got it.* He understood that bodies matter. That rest matters. That carrying things alone was never the plan.

There's a story in Luke's Gospel that is easy to miss, just a handful of verses tucked into a busy chapter, yet it's profound in what it reveals about Jesus and how He honors the body.

Jesus was teaching in a synagogue on the Sabbath when He saw her. A woman, bent over, crippled by a spirit for eighteen long years. Eighteen years. That's almost two decades of looking down. Twenty years of living hunched over, unable to look people in the eye. Her posture shaped her whole existence: the way she carried herself, the way she viewed the world, the way she related to the people around her. Jesus saw her condition and made the first move. "When Jesus saw her, he called her over and said, 'Woman, you are set free from your ailment.' When he laid his hands on her, immediately she stood up straight and began praising God" (Luke 13:12-13).

This is what love looks like in Jesus' hands. Jesus sees. Jesus notices. Jesus responds. In a society where women – especially women who were sick – were often ignored, marginalized, or downright shunned, Jesus reached out His hand. With one touch, He restored her body, her dignity, and her ability to meet the world face-to-face again.

I think about that woman sometimes and wonder how she must have felt when her body finally opened up. When she stood up straight for the first time in nearly two decades, her lungs filling with air she didn't have to fight for. Looking into the faces of others instead of staring at the dust beneath her feet. What must that have felt like?

I can't help but think, *how many of us are hunched over in ways no one can see?* Burdens that bend us down in spirit if not in body. We've adjusted our lives around it. Stopped asking for healing. Stopped imagining things could be different.

Jesus sees you. He sees the way your body tells your story. He notices the places where you've been folded in on yourself. Just like the woman in Luke's gospel, Jesus doesn't wait for you to have the perfect words or the courage to ask. He calls you closer.

> To stand up a little straighter.
>
> To breathe a little deeper.
>
> To live a little less burdened, bent, and bound.
>
> To take one step toward a life that is a little less burdened, a little less bound, a little more free.

This is what Jesus does; He meets you in the posture you've grown accustomed to, and with one word, one touch, He begins to open you up again. What if we began to meet our own bent places with that same tenderness? What if we paused long enough to ask, *What is my body trying to tell me?* Jesus sees the burdens you've adapted to, the pain you've normalized, the way you've learned to keep moving even when it hurts. Still, His invitation remains: *Come closer. Let Me help you stand again.*

Spiritual Practices For Physical Renewal

Your body is a sacred creation. It carries your story, holds your spirit, and reveals what's going on inside. Sometimes it even speaks the truths your soul hasn't yet found words for.

Breath prayers can steady your nervous system and remind you of God's presence. Gentle movement can release the tension you've been storing for years. Journaling can help put into words the emotions your body has been carrying in silence. Silence and stillness can reveal the worries buried beneath your to-do list. Gratitude can shift your body's posture, softening your shoulders and unclenching your heart.

Each of the following practices opens a small, sacred space where you can hear your own heart and welcome God's healing work. Start gently; just one breath, one practice, one honest moment of paying attention at a time.

The One-Minute Body Scan

You can do this anywhere – at your desk, in line at the store, even while waiting for your coffee. No need to close your eyes unless you want to. Here's how:

1. Sit comfortably.
2. Take a slow, deep breath – in through your nose, out through your mouth.
3. Start at the top of your head. Notice any tension in your forehead.
4. Move down to your jaw. Is it clenched? Let it go.
5. Scan down your neck and shoulders. Take another breath. Let them drop.
6. Continue downward: arms, hands, stomach, legs, feet.
7. Wherever you find tension, pause. Breathe. Release.
8. When you've finished, take one more slow breath and thank God for the gift of your body. Whisper, "Lord, I'm listening."

Listening Journal

Sometimes your body knows the truth before your mind does. Journaling gives that truth a safe place to land. Here's how to try it:

1. Set a timer for five minutes.
2. Take a deep breath in through your nose and out through your mouth.
3. Ask yourself: What have I been feeling lately that I haven't said out loud?
4. Write without editing or judging. Allow the words to spill out, even if they don't make sense at first.
5. When the timer goes off, read over what you've written and underline anything that feels important.
6. Offer what you've underlined to Jesus in prayer, "Here it is, Lord", or speak a few sentences asking for help, healing, or direction.
7. Close with three deep breaths, imagining you're inhaling God's peace and exhaling the weight you've been carrying.

This is a space where your body's quiet wisdom can meet God's healing presence.

Gratitude Posture

Gratitude changes your mood and it changes your body. Shoulders relax. Breath deepens. Your heart opens. Here's how to try it:

1. Stand or sit tall, letting your shoulders drop away from your ears.
2. Take a deep breath and, as you exhale, think of one thing you're grateful for today.

3. Speak it out loud or write it down.

4. Picture that gratitude filling your heart and flowing through your body like warmth.

5. Repeat with two more things you're thankful for.

6. As you finish, rest your hands over your heart and breathe deeply, letting gratitude settle into your whole being.

7. End with, "Thank You, Lord, for these gifts. Help me see more."

Gratitude can be a physical act of worship, aligning body and spirit toward God's goodness.

Naming the Weight

Sometimes the heaviness you feel in your body is connected to something your heart has been carrying for a while. This simple practice helps you notice, name, and invite Jesus into those places. Here's how:

1. Take a few slow breaths and gently scan your body.

2. Write down any places that feel tight, heavy, or tired.

3. Next to each, jot down what you think might be connected: stress, grief, fear, over-commitment, etc.

4. Offer a short prayer for each one, inviting Jesus to bring His healing presence there.

5. End with prayer: Come close, Lord, to this place in me that needs Your healing touch.

Sacred Stretching

This simple practice greets your body before the world's demands greet you. You don't need special clothes or equipment, just a few minutes of presence. Here's how to try it:

1. After brushing your teeth (and before reaching for your phone), stand tall.

2. Lift your arms slowly overhead, reaching your fingertips toward the ceiling.

3. Roll your shoulders back in a slow circle, then forward.

4. Tilt your head gently from side to side, noticing the stretch along your neck.

5. Bend forward and reach toward your toes – or your knees – whatever feels right today.

6. Take three deep, unhurried breaths.

That's all. In less than two minutes, you've told your body, "You matter. I'm listening."

Mental Exhaustion

Sometimes even when we finally sit down, we don't actually rest. Our bodies might stop, but our minds keep running, replaying old conversations, worrying about tomorrow, or mentally tackling the to-do list.

There's a name for this, it's called *cognitive load.* It's what happens when you're "off the clock" but still answering just a couple of emails instead. We think we're resting, but our brains are still working overtime.

It's no wonder our minds feel like they never get a moment off duty. We live in a world that is *always on.* Even in the down moments, like standing in line at the store or waiting for the coffee to brew, we reach for our phones, filling every gap with more information, more noise, more to process. Our brains are constantly sifting, sorting, and storing.

It's almost as if our brains have become air traffic control towers – constantly tracking every incoming and outgoing thought, never shutting down the radar. We move from one thing to the next. Even when we're *off,* we're still on – mentally replying to messages or wondering if we remembered to take the chicken out of the freezer.

God didn't wire our brains for constant fragmentation. Dr. Amishi Jha, in her book *Peak Mind,* points out that our attention drifts off-task almost 50% of the time. Which means that in any given moment, we're as likely to be somewhere else mentally as we are to be present. Thinking about dinner while in a meeting. Worrying about that email response while driving. Mentally adding dog food to the grocery list during prayer time. It's become the air we breathe.

Our *busy brain* is not a quirk of modern life. It's a symptom of mental exhaustion that comes from trying to run mental marathons every single day with no finish line in sight. Our brains are like a browser with too many tabs open to count. One holds the email you still haven't sent. Another replays that meeting moment you wish had gone differently. A third asks if you paid the electric bill, while a fourth tries to solve dinner. You click from one to the next, never fully landing anywhere. You're flying back and forth between tabs. A half-finished thought here. A half-hearted attempt to focus there. Little by little, it drains you dry.

Here's the kicker: it doesn't even work. What we call "multitasking" is really just rapid task-switching. Your brain can't actually do two things at the same time; it's wired to focus on one. What we're actually doing is flipping between tasks so fast it feels simultaneous. Like a ping-pong ball, our attention ricochets back and forth, losing steam with every hit.

Your mind wasn't built for constant motion. It was created with rhythm and rest in mind. In Psalm 46:10, God says, "Be still, and know that I am God."

Be still. The two hardest words for a busy brain.

Stillness can feel uncomfortable at first. It can stir up all the thoughts you've been avoiding, all the feelings you've been too busy to name. Stillness asks you to lay down the to-do list and silence the notifications. Yet, stillness is not empty. Stillness is the space where God's voice cuts through the noise. Stillness is full of Jesus' presence. Full of breath. Full of the quiet awareness that the Holy Spirit is near.

Here's the thing – Jesus lived this way. Flip through the Gospels and you won't find Jesus rushing through a marketplace muttering, *I'm behind schedule, people! I've got miracles to perform and parables to preach, let's move it along!* That's not Jesus' way.

Take the story of Jairus' daughter (Mark 5:21-43, Luke 8:40-56). Jairus, a synagogue leader, pushes through a crowd to beg Jesus to come heal his dying child. It's an emergency, the kind of moment we'd treat like sirens-blaring, lights-flashing, drop everything urgency.

Jesus doesn't sprint. He simply walks with Jairus. And then – a delay. A woman in the crowd reaches out and touches the edge of Jesus' cloak. Most of us would keep moving, thinking, *I'll circle back later.* But not Jesus. He stops.

I can only imagine Jairus getting impatient here. *What are You doing? My daughter is dying, and You're stopping for a conversation?*

Jesus doesn't move at the pace of human urgency. He moves at the pace of divine intention. He turns and asks, *"Who touched Me?"* The disciples look around like, *Seriously? Everyone is touching You.* Jesus knew someone had reached out in faith. Someone had poured out their last bit of hope in one desperate grasp. He wasn't going to rush past that moment.

He waits.

He listens.

He gives her space to tell her whole story. Not the condensed version. Not the bullet points. The whole, unfiltered story. In that sacred pause, healing happens. "Daughter, your faith has healed you. Go in peace and be freed from your suffering."

He calls her *daughter.* In one word, Jesus does more than heal her body. He gives her a name. He restores her identity. He claims her as His own and places her back into community. And all of this unfolds while Jairus is still waiting.

Just as Jesus finishes speaking with the woman, word arrives. Jairus' daughter has died. If I were Jairus, I think my heart would have split in two – grief on one side, frustration on the other. I was the one who found Jesus first. I told Him how urgent this was. *Why did He stop? Didn't He understand the clock was ticking?* If only He had hurried. If only He hadn't paused. If only that woman hadn't stepped in.

Jesus turns to Jairus and says, *"Don't be afraid; just believe."* Jesus is not rushed. He's not shaken. He walks to Jairus' house, steps into the room, takes the little girl by the hand, and brings her back to life.

Not hurried.

Not frantic.

Utterly faithful.

This story reminds us that sometimes the miracle happens in the middle. Jesus is never thrown off course by interruptions. In fact, Jesus seems to *expect* them. Jesus models a different way of moving through life. He isn't ruled by schedules or swayed by every voice demanding His attention. Jesus is drawn by need and led by love. He moves at a pace that makes room for mercy. He notices the ones others overlook, hears the cries others have tuned out, and stops where others would rush past. In His presence, nothing is too small to matter. No one is too insignificant to be seen.

Maybe that's our next step, too – to stop rushing through our lists and start watching for God's presence right where we are. If we slow down enough to notice, we begin to see that Jesus has been here all along. We realize the world won't fall apart if we move at the pace of grace. The emails can wait. The laundry can wait. The notifications can wait. But the moment in front of us? The person in front of us? The still, steady voice of God within us? *That can't wait.*

When we choose Jesus' presence over a frantic pace, we trade mental exhaustion for holy attention. We allow our souls to breathe again. And in that breathing space, we just might find the miracle in the middle.

Spiritual Practices for Mental Exhaustion
The One-Minute Mind Reset

You can do this anywhere – at your desk, in the car (while parked), or before you walk into a meeting. No need to close your eyes unless you want to. Here's how:

- Sit comfortably and take a slow, deep breath – in through your nose, out through your mouth.
- Notice what's on your mind right now – worries, to-dos, unfinished conversations.
- Imagine setting each thought down, one by one, like placing books on a shelf.
- If something feels heavy, picture handing it to Jesus.
- Take another slow breath and simply notice the stillness that remains.

When you've finished, take one more deep breath and thank Jesus for the gift of His presence. Offer a simple breath prayer, on the inhale: "Holy Lord," on the exhale, "I am here."

The Two-Minute Breath Prayer

You can do this anywhere – while making your morning coffee, in the grocery store line, or before bed.

Sit or stand comfortably.

Breathe in slowly through your nose as you silently pray, "Be still."

Exhale gently through your mouth as you pray, "and know that You are God."

Repeat this rhythm for 4 to 5 breaths.

Let the words sync with your breath until they become an anchor.

When you've finished, thank Jesus for stilling your mind, praying, "My mind rests in You."

The Three Item Gratitude Shift

You can do this when your thoughts feel scattered or you're stuck in over-thinking.

Pause whatever you're doing.

Name three specific things, big or small, you're grateful for right now.

As you name each one, picture your shoulders softening and your breath slowing.

Allow gratitude to shift your attention away from what's overwhelming toward what is good.

When you've finished, thank Jesus for these gifts, praying, "Lord, my eyes are on Your goodness."

The Mini Sabbath Pause

You can do this any time your brain feels overloaded and you need a reset.

Stop for sixty seconds.

Set down whatever's in your hands, physically or mentally.

Take three slow breaths, imagining the pace of your thoughts slowing down.

Say quietly, "This moment belongs to You, Lord."

Allow that truth to be your resting place before you continue.

When you've finished, pray, *"God, I step forward with Your peace."*

The Three-Second Pause

You can do this before speaking, responding to a message, or stepping into your next task.

Stop for a moment.

Inhale slowly for three seconds.

Exhale gently for three seconds.

Let your shoulders drop and your attention settle into the present.

When you've finished, you might feel led to pray, "Here I am, Lord."

When we hurry from one moment to the next, our minds slip into autopilot, pulling from old patterns, replaying the same thoughts, and reacting out of habit rather than intention.

A pause – even just one slow breath – breaks that cycle. It creates a holy interruption, a small opening where God can speak something new. Scientists might call it a "pattern interrupt." We can call it *grace making room for possibility.*

Before you answer a question, pause – Lord, help me respond with love.

Before you open your email, pause – Jesus, be present in this space.

Before you step out the door, pause – God, let me carry Your peace with me today.

Mindful Transitions: The Two-Minute Rule

Lately, I've been practicing something simple that's made a surprising difference. It's called the Two-Minute Rule. Every time you transition from one task to the next, you stop for two minutes.

Two minutes to breathe. Two minutes to reset. Two minutes to let go of whatever you were just carrying so you can arrive fully in what's next.

Our days are filled with rapid task-switching – email to text, meeting to errand – without a single breath in between. By lunchtime, our minds are cluttered, our nerves frayed. The Two-Minute Rule is like gently closing one mental tab at a time. It gives your brain permission to exhale, release what's done, and open up space for what's ahead. Here's how to practice:

When you finish a task, give yourself two full minutes before starting the next one.

Done with emails? Two minutes.

Just unloaded the groceries? Two minutes.

Wrapped up a phone call? Two minutes.

It's that simple. Long enough to create space. Short enough to feel doable.

Close your eyes, if you'd like, and take a slow, deep breath. Inhale for a count of four – hold for two – exhale for four. Feel the air expand your lungs, loosening the tight places. As you breathe out, picture yourself letting go of whatever came before, clearing room for what's next.

The Evening Examen – Mental Decluttering Before Sleep

Before you turn off the light, maybe after brushing your teeth and plugging in your phone, take three unhurried minutes.

1. Settle In. Sit comfortably. Breathe deeply. Close your eyes if it helps you focus.

2. Review the Day with God. Slowly walk back through your day, from morning to now. Where did you notice God's presence? Where did you feel distant or distracted? What lingers in your mind – unfinished conversations, replayed moments, unspoken worries?

3. Release and Rest. Name each thing weighing on you – worries, regrets, "I should have" moments. Imagine placing them into Jesus' hands, trusting He will hold them through the night.

4. Close in Gratitude.

Pray, "Thank You, Lord, for being here today. Be with me as I rest." Take one last slow breath and let it go, knowing tomorrow is in God's care.

Emotional Exhaustion

Psychologists call it *emotional over-functioning.* It's that reflex to step in, smooth things over, and keep the peace whether or not anyone asked you to. Family argument starting to bubble? You're already the referee. Tension at work? You're drafting the perfectly worded email to fix it. A friend sends a text with even a hint of frustration? You're already halfway down a *Google* rabbit hole looking for solutions before they've finished typing.

Dr. Brené Brown, a researcher known for her work on vulnerability, courage, and emotional well-being, describes over-functioning as a kind of *emotional-armor*. In her book *The Gifts of Imperfection,* she explains that it's what we put on when we feel uncertain, anxious, or afraid but don't want anyone to know. Instead of sitting with those feelings, we spring into action. We fix. We manage. We control.

Over-functioning convinces us that it's our job to fix, manage, and control everyone else's emotional world, too. We become walking triage units, moving from one relational emergency to the next. Someone's upset? We're already thinking of what to say to calm them down. A conversation turns tense? We rush to smooth it over before it turns south. A misunderstanding happens? We're halfway through composing the perfect text or email to make sure everyone leaves with their feelings intact. We carry around an emotional first aid kit, ready to patch up every hurt, every misunderstanding, every tense conversation. While that sounds noble, it's exhausting. Holding it all together is a full-time job, and I'm guessing it's not the one you signed up for.

There's also a hidden cost. Armor is heavy. It slows your steps. It makes it harder to rest. You forget what it feels like to walk freely, to move without the constant burden of holding everything together. Over time, this constant scanning for problems to solve leaves us mentally frayed, physically tense, and spiritually weary. We start living in a state of low-grade anxiety, always on alert, always prepared for the next fire to put out.

God created our minds with stunning complexity; a place where thoughts, feelings, ideas, and memories live side by side. And there's a limit. It's like a suitcase that you keep shoving more into. At first it's manageable. Then you start squeezing in one last shirt, one last pair of shoes, one more *just in case* item. Eventually, you can't zip it no matter how hard you try. The problem isn't the suitcase. *It's the weight you're asking it to hold.*

Our minds work the same way: designed for capacity, not for carrying everything indefinitely. Our minds and hearts can hold extraordinary amounts of empathy. God designed our hearts to beat in rhythm with others, to show kindness and share in their pain. When we take on the unofficial role of emotional project manager for everyone around us, absorbing their stress, fixing their conflicts, and carrying their burdens as if they were our own, we're stuffing more and more into that emotional suitcase. Eventually, the seams stretch, the zipper sticks, and the weight becomes impossible to carry.

Dr. Bessel van der Kolk, in his ground-breaking work *The Body Keeps the Score*, dismantles one of the biggest myths about stress and emotional pain: that if we just push it aside, bury it deep enough, or distract ourselves long enough, it will disappear on its own. That's not how we're designed. His research shows that our bodies keep a kind of living record of what we've been through. Stress, trauma, and unprocessed grief don't simply vanish when our minds decide to move on; instead, they lodge themselves in our nervous system, muscles, and even our posture, influencing how we feel and how we live.

Picture your body as a calm pond. Then *plunk*, a pebble drops. The initial impact may seem small – a frustrating meeting, a conflict with a friend, or a hurtful comment. The splash is small, over in a moment; however, underneath, the ripples spread. The ripples travel through your nervous system, tightening your chest, tensing your jaw, or knotting your shoulders. Days later, you may not even remember what set it in motion. Your mind might not remember every detail, but your body does.

The body has a remarkable memory. It collects every unprocessed hurt and every bit of tension you've pushed aside, and it doesn't easily let go. Dr. van der Kolk calls this *neuroception*. This is your nervous system's ability to scan the world for danger without your conscious permission. It's automatic. This is a gift when you're in real danger. If your body has stored past trauma or lives with ongoing stress, this system stays switched on, like a smoke alarm that never stops beeping. You stay in a state of readiness – tense, alert, and waiting for the next shoe to drop – even when you're at rest.

This unrelenting state of alert can take a toll. Research shows that staying in protection mode for too long can contribute to chronic anxiety, depression, digestive issues, heart problems, and even autoimmune conditions. Why? Because your body is designed to respond to short bursts of danger, then return to a state of safety. When that reset never comes, your nervous system keeps pumping out stress hormones, tightening muscles, and rerouting energy toward survival instead of restoration.

The same body that remembers pain also carries the remarkable capacity to heal. Just as stress and hurt can be stored deep within your nervous system, they can also be released. Your body is more than a container for your experiences; it's an active participant in your restoration. When you engage in practices like slow, intentional breathwork, gentle stretching, or even sitting in stillness, you're sending a message to your nervous system: *It's safe to relax now.* Bit by bit, these small acts of care allow your body to shift out of high alert and into a state of repair.

Dr. van der Kolk reminds us that healing happens when we learn to inhabit our bodies again, in ways that feel safe and supported. This is why embodied practices like yoga, mindful walking, breath prayers, and even creative expression can help untangle knots of tension that have been held for years. These practices give your body permission to process what your mind has been carrying, to release the weight you've been holding, and to make space for peace.

I'm reminded of Jesus standing at the tomb of His friend Lazarus. He knew resurrection was only moments away. He knew death wouldn't have the final word. And still, Jesus wept. The Greek word in John 11:35, *dakruo*, carries the sense of deep, gut-level sorrow. Jesus didn't sidestep His grief or rush to the happy ending. He let His body feel the weight of loss. His tears honored the ache, giving space for both the pain of the moment and the hope to come.

We see it again when Jesus looks out over Jerusalem and weeps for a city wandering far from God's heart (Luke 19:41). He doesn't push His compassion aside or tell Himself to "be strong." He pauses. He mourns. He allows His love for His people to take up space in His body. In His eyes, in His voice, in the tears streaming down His face.

Jesus shows us that being fully alive in God's presence means being fully present to our emotions. He gives us permission to let our bodies tell the truth, to honor our sorrow, and to allow both pain and love to be felt deeply.

Then there was the Garden of Gethsemane, where the weight of what was coming weighed so heavily on Jesus that His sweat fell like drops of blood (Luke 22:44). He didn't hide His anguish. He didn't push it down or pretend He was fine. Jesus brought it – raw and unfiltered – before the Father. In that garden, Jesus allowed His body to speak the truth of His soul. Every trembling breath, every drop of sweat was an embodied prayer. He didn't bypass the pain. He moved through it. He stayed present to it. Jesus shows us that there is holiness in listening to your body's signals, in naming your grief, and in letting yourself fully feel what's there. The way through sorrow isn't in rushing past it, it's in holding space for it, just as Jesus did.

The miracle is this: when you honor your body's signals – when you pause, listen, and respond – you create space for release. You interrupt the unconscious habit of tucking stress and unspoken sadness deep into your bones. You make room for grace to enter, for healing to take root.

This is slow work. Gentle work. It takes patience and practice. It's learning to notice where it hurts, where tension shows up, where tightness finds a home. It's choosing to let your body speak its truth without rushing to silence it.

This is where wholeness begins. Right here, in the tender act of tending to the places that ache. In breathing deeply enough to ask: *What is my body trying to tell me?* And then, in love, listening for the answer.

Spiritual Practices for Emotional Exhaustion

These next practices are designed to help you pause long enough to notice what your heart is holding, to invite Jesus into it, and to release what you were never meant to carry alone. They're not about "fixing" your emotions, instead, they give them a safe place to be heard and held in Jesus' presence.

The Hand-to-Heart Pause

You can do this when you feel weighed down by someone else's emotions, or when you've been "holding it all together" for too long.

> Sit or stand comfortably.
>
> Place one hand over your heart and the other on your belly.
>
> Breathe in slowly through your nose, feeling both hands rise.
>
> As you exhale, offer a short prayer. "Lord, I give You what is not mine to carry."
>
> Repeat for 4 to 5 breaths, letting your shoulders soften with each exhale.
>
> When you've finished, pray: "Holy Spirit, fill me with Your peace."

The Emotional Release Breath

You can do this anytime emotions feel stuck: after a hard conversation, a stressful meeting, or a moment of disappointment.

Sit somewhere you feel safe.

Inhale deeply through your nose for four counts.

Exhale with an audible sigh, imagining the weight leaving your body.

On the next inhale, silently pray: "Jesus, receive this." On the exhale: "I release it to You."

Repeat 3 to 5 times, allowing the breath to carry away what you no longer need to hold.

The Safe Space Visualization

You can do this when you've been in a tense environment or after absorbing too much of others' stress.

Close your eyes and imagine a place where you feel deeply safe, perhaps by still water, in a sunlit room, or wrapped in a warm blanket.

Picture Jesus there with you. Notice His calm. His nearness.

Breathe slowly, letting His presence create a protective boundary around your heart.

When you've finished, thank Him for being your refuge, "Lord, You are my safe place."

The Compassion Reset

You can do this when you're overwhelmed by empathy and it's tipping into over-responsibility.

Pause whatever you're doing.

Place both hands open in front of you.

Picture holding the person or situation you're concerned about in your palms.

Gently lift your hands upward, releasing them into Jesus' care and praying, "Lord, love them even more than I can."

Breathe in Jesus' compassion for you; breathe out His compassion for them.

The Three-Feeling Check-In

You can do this when you've been running on autopilot, unaware of your emotional state. Pause for a moment and ask yourself:

What am I feeling right now?

Where do I feel it in my body?

What do I need from Jesus in this moment?

Name your top three emotions without judgment or overthinking.

Pray, Lord, meet me here.

Take three deep breaths, inviting Jesus' presence into each emotion.

The Evening Examen for the Heart

Before bed, set aside a few quiet minutes. Sit comfortably, close your eyes, and take three slow breaths. Review the day with God. Walk through the day's moments, paying attention to where you felt emotionally full and where you felt drained.

Where did you give away more than you could afford?

Where did you feel seen and cared for?

Where did you try to carry more than God asked you to?

Next, release and rest. Imagine placing each emotional burden into Jesus' open hands. If it helps, picture Jesus carrying them to a place where you no longer have to keep watch over them.

Close in gratitude, praying, "Thank You, Lord, for carrying me and what I could not carry myself. Be with me as I rest." Breathe in Jesus' peace.

The Non-Dominant Hand Practice: Writing Past Your Defenses

Sometimes the truest parts of our story hide beneath layers of logic, habit, and self-protection. We might feel the pull to express what's inside; however, our mind quickly edits, explains, or dismisses it. That's why the *Non-Dominant Hand Practice* can be such a profound doorway into deeper healing.

When you pick up a pen with your non-dominant hand, you instantly interrupt your brain's usual patterns. Your dominant side, the part that's practiced, precise, and in control, has to step back. In its place, the more intuitive, creative, and emotionally attuned part of your brain takes the lead. This shift makes space for thoughts and feelings that might not surface in your normal, polished handwriting. Here's how to try it:

Sit somewhere quiet with a notebook or piece of paper. Place the pen in your non-dominant hand and ask a simple question, perhaps, *"What am I feeling right now?"* or *"Lord, what do You want to show me?"* Then write, without worrying about grammar, spelling, or neatness. Allow the words to flow exactly as they come.

Dr. Lucia Capacchione, who pioneered this method in expressive arts therapy, found that people often uncovered hidden memories, unspoken griefs, longings, or even unexpected joys through this process. You might be surprised by what surfaces; truths your heart has been holding quietly for a long time.

As you write, invite Jesus to be present in the process. Imagine Him sitting beside you, listening without judgment, holding whatever surfaces with tenderness. When you're finished, pause and pray, "Lord, thank You for meeting me here. Help me hold these truths with grace." This practice makes space for the parts of you that rarely get the mic.

Relational Exhaustion

Some of the deepest exhaustion doesn't come from what you do, it comes from who you're with. Have you ever walked away from a conversation feeling like someone just drained the battery out of your soul? Or maybe you left a family gathering, climbed into your car, and just sat there – hands on the wheel, eyes closed – whispering a prayer for strength before you even turned the key? Nothing drains us faster than relationships that are heavy, complicated, or hard to navigate. Strained relationships take more out of us than any overbooked calendar ever could. They hijack our mental space, keep us awake at night, and follow us into the next room, the next conversation, the next day. The harder they are to navigate, the more energy they steal and the less we have left for the things and people who refill us.

Start by tuning in to the quiet signals your body and spirit are sending you. Sometimes we ignore them because we're *supposed to*; however, those subtle cues are often the first sign that something in a relationship is out of balance.

Notice the tension. Does your stomach knot up, your shoulders tighten, or your jaw clench when you see their name pop up on your phone? That's your body bracing for impact before a single word is spoken.

Notice the mental rehearsals. Do you find yourself running through possible conversations in your head before you meet or replaying what was said long after you've parted? That's your mind trying to control or make sense of something that feels emotionally risky or unresolved.

Notice your energy shift. Do you walk away feeling heavier, smaller, or more depleted, even if nothing overtly went wrong? That's your spirit signaling that the exchange cost you more than it replenished.

These are holy indicators, God-given warning lights on the dashboard of your soul telling you that a relationship may be taking more than it's giving. Learning to notice and name these cues is a step in reclaiming the space needed for love to flow more freely. You can begin making small, intentional choices to protect your energy and honor your well-being. Guarding your heart creates healthy, loving boundaries that allow relationships to grow without depleting you. Sometimes that means adapting how and when you engage, rather than walking away entirely.

Pause before you respond. When a call or text comes in, remember: the buzz of your phone is not a command. It's simply an invitation, and you have the right to choose when (and if) to accept it. Before you reach for your phone, let it ring or vibrate one extra time. Use those few seconds to notice your body: are your shoulders tight, is your stomach tense, is your mind already rehearsing what to say? Ask yourself, *Am I in a place – mentally, emotionally, spiritually – where I can be fully present right now?* If the answer is no, it's okay to let the call go to voicemail or to wait until you have a quieter moment to reply to that text. You might even send a quick message: "Hey, I'm not able to talk right now, but I'll call you back later today." or "I want to give you my full attention. Can we talk in an hour?" By pausing, you give yourself the gift of choice. You're no longer reacting out of habit or obligation; you're responding out of intention and peace. Given enough time, this simple practice can turn what used to be draining exchanges into more grounded, meaningful conversations.

Set gentle limits around time and topics. Some conversations feel like open-ended hallways. You walk in and suddenly realize there's no clear way out. When certain relationships have a history of spiraling into negativity, gossip, or conflict, you can lovingly place gentle guardrails around how long you stay and what you talk about. Before you begin, decide how much time you can give while still leaving yourself energy for the rest of your day. You might think, *I can be fully present for 20 minutes, but after that, I'll start to feel drained.* Set a timer on your phone if it helps. Create a natural "exit point" by saying, "I only have about 15 minutes, but I'm glad to connect."

Steer the conversation toward life-giving topics. If you know certain subjects are land mines, be ready with a few uplifting questions or neutral topics to move toward. For example: "Before I forget, how did your garden turn out this year?" "I wanted to tell you about something I read in Scripture this morning, it made me think of you." If the conversation takes a sharp turn into draining territory, it's okay to redirect or wrap it up. You might say: "I hear that's weighing on you, and I want to give it more thought. Let's pick this up another time." "I've really enjoyed catching up, but I need to get going now." This redirect honors the relationship by keeping it in a space where you can show up with love instead of resentment.

Name what strengthens the relationship. Sometimes people simply don't realize what's hard for us. We often assume people know what strengthens or strains a relationship, and most of us aren't mind readers. Clear, compassionate communication is a gift both to you and to them. Affirm what works. Let the other person know the things they do that genuinely fill your cup. For example: "I love when we share good news with each other first, it makes me feel so connected to you." "When we pray together before we hang up, I feel encouraged for the rest of the day." Focus on your feelings rather than their faults. Swap "You always…" for "I feel…" or "I need…." For instance: Instead of, "You're always negative." Try, "I feel heavy when our conversations focus only on problems. Could we also share what's going well?"

Sometimes the best shift happens when you make it collaborative. "When we focus on encouraging each other, I feel closer to you. What do you think about ending each call with something we're grateful for?" "I've noticed I do better when we keep our calls to about 30 minutes. Could we try that so I can give you my best energy?" When you name what's helpful, you're opening a shared conversation about how to love each other well. You'll experience rhythms that bring life to both of you.

Plan recovery time. Plan your recovery like you would any other important appointment. If you know a conversation or gathering will be emotionally heavy, block out time afterward for something that refills you: a few minutes of quiet prayer, a slow walk in fresh air, your favorite play list on repeat, or coffee with someone who makes you laugh. Just like a runner needs a cool down, your soul needs space to breathe.

Healthy boundaries are not walls to keep people out; they're gates that allow love, grace, and peace to flow both ways without leaving you empty. Walls shut everything out. Gates, on the other hand, open and close with wisdom. They let in what is life-giving and protect you from what is depleting. A healthy gate swings open to kindness, truth, and mutual care, and it also closes gently when criticism turns cutting, when demands outweigh respect, or when the interaction overwhelms your spirit. Boundaries give relationships structure and safety, making it possible to remain open-hearted without becoming overextended. In God's design, boundaries steward your soul so you can keep loving well without burning out.

Reflection Questions: Noticing and Navigating Relational Drains

Think about the last few conversations or interactions that left you feeling emotionally tired.

What was it about those moments that felt heavy?

Were there recurring topics, tones, or dynamics that contributed to the drain?

What physical cues does your body give you when you're heading into (or coming out of) a draining interaction?

Do your shoulders tense? Does your breathing change? Do you feel fatigued, even if it's early in the day?

Which relationships in your life feel most life-giving right now?

What is it about those interactions that replenishes your energy? How might you invite more of those qualities into other relationships?

How do you typically respond when your phone buzzes or a message pops up from someone who drains your energy?

Do you react immediately out of habit? Or do you pause and check in with God and yourself before responding?

Where might you need to set a gentle boundary this week to protect your emotional and spiritual health?

What might that boundary look like in action? How could you communicate it with kindness and clarity?

After a difficult interaction, what practices help you come back to center in God's peace? Which of these practices could you plan ahead as "recovery time" after your next hard conversation?

Your "Yes" Costs More Than You Realize

One of the sneakiest culprits of relational exhaustion is over-giving. Let me be clear: giving is good. Generosity is holy. Jesus Himself calls us to lay down our lives for others, to serve, to love without keeping score. There's a difference between pouring out from a full well and draining yourself dry.

When you are constantly meeting needs, showing up, carrying the emotional load, or making sure everyone else is okay without ever pausing to be poured into, it's like running your car on fumes and wondering why you can't make it up the next hill.

At first, you ignore the signs, thinking a quick refill of rest or a slower week ahead will solve it. When the pace doesn't let up, your "yes" starts to come from habit instead of health. Your giving stops feeling like a joyful offering and starts feeling like a survival strategy. You say "yes" because it's what you've always done, because you don't want to disappoint, because it feels easier than saying no. Deep down, you know this isn't sustainable. You can't pour living water from a dry well.

Dr. Brené Brown calls it *the hustle for worthiness,* that exhausting undercurrent that drives so many of us to keep showing up, saying yes, and all tied to the unspoken belief that our value is directly tied to our availability. Most of the time, we don't even realize it's there.

If I'm always available, maybe I'll prove I'm dependable.

If I say yes to every request, maybe they'll see I'm valuable.

If I keep the peace and make sure no one is disappointed, maybe, just maybe, they'll love me. It's a subtle but powerful lie: my worth depends on my usefulness to others.

The danger is that this way of living turns love into a ledger. Generosity becomes currency; something you spend to buy acceptance. You keep swiping the card, and before long, the account is overdrawn.

Dr. Brown's research points to a sobering truth: many of us, especially women, have been conditioned to believe that *more* is the mark of love and value. More helpful. More available. More self-sacrificing. Somewhere along the way, we heard that our worth is measured in how much of ourselves we give away. If we can just do a little more, be a little more, give a little more, maybe then we'll finally be enough.

Here's the painful irony, when we keep pouring from a place of emptiness, we're not truly giving; we're depleting. It's like trying to water a garden from a dry well; the harder you pump, the less you have to offer until there's nothing left but dust. No matter how much we give from scarcity, it will never be enough to fill the hole we're trying to patch. Because the need we're trying to meet, the deep desire to be seen, known, and loved, can't be earned through constant output. It's a gift we can only receive, rooted in the unshakable truth that our value comes from God, not from how much of ourselves we burn away for others.

Dr. Brown's research also reveals something we don't often discuss, *over-functioning isn't just exhausting; it's profoundly isolating.* When you're always the one holding everything together, you quietly send the message, sometimes without realizing it, that you don't need help. People get used to leaning on you, but rarely think to lean *with* you.

Here's the hidden cost: you stop letting others show up for you. You become so accustomed to carrying more than your share of the load that you forget what it's like to rest in someone else's care. You miss out on the give-and-take that makes relationships rich and resilient. In the process, you unintentionally rob others of something important too – the chance to grow, to contribute, to experience the beauty of mutuality. Relationships become lopsided because your partner's never been invited into the work of loving you back.

This creates a quiet loneliness. You can be surrounded by people, needed by everyone, and still feel unseen. The heartbreaking truth is that over-functioning often grows from the soil of fear. Fear that if you stop, everything will fall apart. Fear that if you say no, you'll be replaced or forgotten. Fear that if you're not everything to everyone, you'll somehow be nothing to anyone.

Dr. Brown tells us that healing from the hustle for worthiness begins with two unshakable realities. First: you are worthy of love and belonging exactly as you are, in this moment, before you lift a finger or check a box. Second: you do not have to earn rest. Your worth is not measured by your productivity. Your value is not defined

by your availability. You are allowed to be loved even when you're not "useful."
You are allowed to take up space even when you're still. You are allowed to rest as a
rhythm of grace birthed into the life God intends for you.

Jesus Loved Without Losing Himself

There's a striking moment in Scripture where Jesus models loving without losing
Himself in Mark 1:36-38. The day before, He had healed many in Capernaum:
casting out demons, restoring the sick, pouring Himself out for hours. By morning,
word had spread. A crowd had gathered again, arriving with expectation. The
disciples went looking for Jesus and found Him praying alone. Breathless, they
blurted out, "Everyone is looking for you!"

I imagine their urgency. *Jesus, you're in demand! The people are here! You're
changing lives, how can we stop now?*

If that were you or me, we might have felt the pressure to meet every need. The tug
of obligation. The fear of letting someone down. Most of us would have grabbed our
things and rushed to the crowd, apologizing for stepping away. Yet, Jesus didn't rush
back. Instead, He looked at His disciples and said "Let us go on to the neighboring
towns, so that I may proclaim the message there also; for that is what I came out
to do." Wait, *what?* People were still waiting. People who hadn't been healed yet.
People who had traveled miles for a glimpse of hope. And yet, Jesus walked away.
Not because He didn't care. Not because their needs weren't real. Instead, because
Jesus was clear about His calling. Jesus' "yes" flowed from God's direction, not from
the demands of the crowd.

Jesus said no to good things so Jesus could say yes to the right things.

Jesus teaches us something here that's both freeing and deeply challenging.
Love does not require you to meet every need. Compassion does not mean constant
availability. While healing bodies was a beautiful and compassionate part of His
ministry, it wasn't Jesus' ultimate purpose. His mission was far greater: to bring the
Kingdom of God near, to proclaim the good news, to invite hearts into a relationship
with God. Every miracle, every teaching, every step pointed to that mission. That's
why Jesus could walk away from the crowds still waiting to be healed. Jesus had
clarity and He refused to be pulled off course, even by good and noble things. That's
the difference: Jesus knew when to say "no" to a good thing in order to say "yes" to
the *right* thing.

This is the kind of wisdom we're invited to practice, too. Learning to slow down
enough to notice what really matters. It's the Spirit's gentle guidance that helps us
tell the difference between what feels urgent and what is actually ours to do. It's
being able to hear the loud noise of other people's expectations and still recognize

God's quiet voice leading us. Without that kind of clarity, we'll keep saying "yes" to everything. Even the good things – until we're completely spent.

How often do we say "yes" just because something is good? A project at work that could use our skills. A volunteer role that really does make a difference. A community event that feels too important to skip. One yes at a time, our days and calendars fill up with good, worthwhile things. Somewhere along the way, we realize that in saying "yes" to everything good, we may have unintentionally been saying "no" to the things that are *right* for us in this season. The things that keep us healthy, rooted, and connected to God's call on our life right now.

I can't even count the number of times I've said "yes" when everything in me was thinking *no*. Yes to joining the committee. Yes to the favor that was supposed to "only take a few minutes" but somehow swallowed my entire afternoon. Why did I say "yes?" Because I didn't want to seem unhelpful. Because I thought I should. Because I was afraid of disappointing someone. Maybe even afraid they'd think less of me if I said "no."

Jesus didn't apologize for leaving Capernaum. He didn't over-explain His decision. He didn't try to squeeze in "just one more" miracle before heading out. He simply said, "This is why I came," and moved on in step with God.

Imagine the freedom of living like that. Moving through your day with a steady and holy confidence that your yes is rooted in Jesus' call for you, and your no is just as holy.

No guilt.

No scrambling.

No proving.

Just a deep assurance that you are where you are meant to be, doing what you are meant to do. This is the way of Jesus. This is the invitation in front of you.

Learning to live this way takes practice. It's not a one-time decision; it's a daily rhythm of listening and responding, again and again. These next practices are designed to help you slow down, tune in to God's voice, and start shaping a life that reflects that same Spirit-led freedom.

Spiritual Practices for Holy Restraint

These next practices are here to help you discover what a Spirit-shaped yes and a holy no look like in your own life. They're about creating breathing room. The kind of space where you can hear Jesus' invitation more clearly and minimize letting every demand set the course. You'll practice pausing before you respond, listening for God's gentle direction, and letting go of the pressure to keep everyone happy.

Over time, you'll enjoy a deeper sense of alignment with God's rhythm for your life.

The Pause Before the Yes

Use this anytime an invitation, request, or opportunity comes your way, especially if your instinct is to respond immediately.

1. When the request is made, resist the urge to answer on the spot.

2. Place both feet flat on the floor. Rest your hands open in your lap.

3. Breathe in for a slow count of four, silently praying, "Lord, is this mine?"

4. Exhale for a count of six, releasing any pressure to decide right now.

5. Ask yourself:

   Does this align with my God-given purpose in this season?

   Do I have the capacity to say yes without sacrificing my health or calling?

   Is this Spirit-led, or is it driven by guilt, fear, or people-pleasing?

6. When ready, respond truthfully, whether your answer is yes, not now, or no, and trust that your no can be as Spirit-honoring as your yes.

Creating Margin for God's Voice

Jesus often withdrew to quiet places to pray and recalibrate. What would it look like for you to create that kind of space too? These are gentle invitations to breathe, to listen, to simply be with Jesus in the middle of all the noise.

1. Once a day, turn off all distractions for 10 minutes: no phone, no emails, no background noise.

2. Sit comfortably, breathe slowly, and let your thoughts settle.

3. Ask Jesus: "What do You want me to say 'yes' to? What do You want me to release?"

4. Notice any nudges, words, or feelings that arise, and write them down.

5. End with gratitude, trusting that even in silence God is speaking.

The "Not Mine to Carry" Release

Use this practice whenever you feel pressed down by other people's expectations or the weight of urgency.

1. Find a comfortable position, standing or sitting.

2. Close your eyes and notice what feels heavy: a responsibility, a task, a conversation, even a relationship that's weighing on your heart.

3. Imagine holding that burden in your hands. Then picture Jesus standing before you, His hands open and ready.

4. Gently place what you're holding into His hands.

5. Whisper (or simply think), "This is Yours, Lord. Show me what is mine to carry and what I can release."

6. Take three slow, deep breaths. With each exhale, imagine the weight lifting, your shoulders softening, your spirit becoming lighter.

Boundary Prayer Walk

Try this practice anytime you feel scattered or unsure about your priorities.

1. Take a slow, mindful walk, whether it's around your house, through your neighborhood, or in a quiet hallway at work.

2. With each step, imagine the Holy Spirit gently marking out healthy boundaries for your time, your energy, and your calling.

3. Pray as you walk: "Lord, guard my yes. Strengthen my no."

4. As you come to the end of your walk, pause. Thank Jesus for shaping your days with purpose and ask Him to guide your steps so they stay in rhythm with His love and direction.

The Holy "No" Rehearsal

Sometimes we need practice saying no in a way that is both honest and kind.

Write down a request you've struggled to turn down in the past.

Pray for wisdom and for the person who asked.

Out loud, practice saying:

"Thank you for thinking of me. I can't take this on right now. That's a great opportunity. It's not mine to carry in this season. I'm honored you asked. I need to say no so I can stay faithful to my other commitments."

Repeat these phrases until they begin to feel natural on your tongue.

Close with a prayer, "Lord, help my no protect the yes You've given me."

Evening Reflection

This evening practice helps you pay attention to where you honored your God-given limits and where you may have stepped past them.

Before bed, take three slow, deep breaths and let the day settle.

Ask yourself, *Where did I say yes today that felt in step with God's leading? Where did I say "yes" even though I sensed a quiet nudge to say "no?" Did I make room for rest and renewal?*

Gently release any misplaced yeses into Jesus' care, trusting Him to carry what is not yours.

Ask Him to guide tomorrow's decisions so that they grow out of peace, not pressure.

End with gratitude, praying: "Thank You, Lord, for leading me today. Keep teaching me to walk in Your rhythm."

Spiritual Exhaustion

Spiritual exhaustion is a weariness that goes deeper than your calendar or your body. It's different from emotional exhaustion, which often comes from strained relationships, or physical burnout, which comes from pushing your body too hard. It's an emptiness where you feel far from God, even if no one around you would ever guess. It's feeling like the well inside you has run dry; where you feel disconnected from the very Source of life: God.

I've been there. I remember seasons when I sat in church and sang the words but my heart felt miles away. Or when I opened my Bible, read the passage, closed it and realized I couldn't remember a single thing I'd just read. My prayers sounded fine out loud, yet inside I wondered, *Is God even hearing this*? Somewhere along the way, I started running on autopilot. That's spiritual exhaustion. And it's more common than you think.

Spiritual exhaustion can look like:

Praying while feeling like no one is listening.

Feeling resentful, numb, or too tired to care.

Showing up for everyone else while your own soul feels neglected.

Wondering why you can't sense Jesus the way you used to or questioning if you've ever really felt His presence at all.

If that's where you are, you're not alone and you're not broken. Your soul is simply inviting you to slow down, pay attention, and rediscover the God who has never stopped loving you.

When your soul feels worn out, it's easy to grab for quick fixes. Take a day off, sleep in, drop a couple of commitments. And honestly? Those things do help. They give your body a break and your mind a little room to breathe. However, if the weariness goes deeper – if it's coming from the inside-out – no amount of rearranging your calendar will bring the energy you're longing for. That's because there's a difference between relief and renewal.

Relief soothes the surface for a little while. Renewal goes straight to the root. Relief is like a cold drink of water when you're thirsty. Refreshing, but temporary. Renewal is finding the spring that never runs dry.

Relief helps you catch your breath.

Renewal teaches you how to breathe again.

To move toward that kind of deep renewal, we start by clearing away the false beliefs that keep us spinning our wheels. Spiritual exhaustion is often misunderstood, and the stories we tell ourselves about it can leave us working harder instead of resting deeper. The next section will gently name those misconceptions so we can finally stop striving and start leaning into the kind of life Jesus promised us.

Misconception #1: "If I were more faithful, I wouldn't feel this way."

It's easy to think that if we just had more faith, we wouldn't feel so worn down. Even the most faithful people in Scripture had dry seasons.

David poured out his anguish in the Psalms. Elijah collapsed under a broom tree, too exhausted to keep going. Jeremiah wept under the weight of his calling.

Their faith wasn't proven by constant joy or perfect energy. It showed up in their honesty with God. They didn't pretend to be okay. They brought their weariness into God's presence.

Faithfulness doesn't mean living on a nonstop spiritual high. It means continuing to turn toward Jesus even when you don't feel Him. It means trusting that the dry places are invitations to lean on Jesus more deeply. Sometimes the most faithful prayer is as simple as: "Lord, I'm tired, and I'm still here."

Misconception #2: "Spiritual exhaustion means I've failed God."

God is not disappointed in you for being weary. Being human is tiring in body, mind, and soul. Your spiritual fatigue is a signal. A holy alarm bell that says your soul needs refilling. God already knows how tired you are. Jesus simply invites you closer, "Come to me, all you who are weary and burdened, and I will give you rest" (Matthew 11:28). Feeling spiritually tired is your invitation to pause, breathe, and receive. To let Jesus meet you right where you are.

Misconception #3: "I just need to try harder."

This might be the sneakiest lie of all: the idea that the way to feel close to Jesus again is to do more. Read more. Pray more. Serve more. Here's the truth: spiritual exhaustion rarely heals by adding more to the list. A tired soul doesn't need a busier schedule; it needs connection with Jesus. When we're constantly doing, we often miss the stillness where renewal happens. What if instead of asking, *"What else should I do?"* you began asking, *"Where can I create space for Jesus to restore me?"*

That space might look like:
A slow, unhurried walk.
A Sabbath nap.

A few honest journal lines about what's on your mind.

Ten minutes of just breathing in Jesus' presence.

Remember, Sabbath was God's fourth commandment. (Exodus 20) Jesus invites you to step off the treadmill of performance and rest in the truth that His love is not earned. It's already yours.

Spiritual Practices For a Weary Soul

These practices are deep breaths for your spirit. Small, intentional pauses that make room for grace to do its quiet work. They help you notice the presence of Jesus already surrounding you and remind you that renewal doesn't have to be rushed. God's love meets you right where you are, not where you think you "should" be.

The Soul Check-In

This practice is for the moments when something inside feels unsettled, but you can't quite put words to it.

Find a quiet space where you can simply be. Sit comfortably, with your feet resting on the ground and your hands open, a posture of receiving.

Take a slow, deep breath in for a count of four, praying in your heart, *Lord, here I am.* Exhale for a count of six, releasing the pressure to have it all figured out.

When you feel ready, ask yourself:

How is my soul? Really?

Where have I felt most alive this week? Where have I felt most drained?

In what moments have I sensed Jesus near? When have I felt distant?

Allow room for your honest thoughts to rise to the surface and jot them down without judgment and editing. Receive them as invitations to deeper conversation with Jesus, who already knows and lovingly holds all that you bring.

The Gentle Reset

This practice is for the times when you're engaging in spiritual exercises like praying, reading Scripture or showing up for worship and still feel far from Jesus.

Set aside 10 unrushed minutes just for you and Jesus. Turn off the noise. Silence your phone, close your laptop, let this time be free of interruptions. Light a candle or pause at a window, letting this moment signal that you are stepping onto sacred ground.

Pray slowly, from the heart, *Lord, draw me close again. I want to know You, not just serve You.*

Choose a short passage of Scripture. Psalm 23, Matthew 11:28-30, or John 15:4

are beautiful places to begin. Read it slowly, letting each word settle before you move on. Sit with it long enough to ask, *Jesus, what are You offering me in this moment?*

When you feel ready, place your hand gently over your heart. Breathe deeply and thank Jesus for being near, even when you cannot always feel it.

The Burden Exchange

This practice is for the days when everything feels heavy – the expectations, the responsibilities, the weight you can't put down.

Find a still moment and close your eyes. Picture yourself holding the weight you've been carrying – the meetings, the worries, the unspoken pressure. See yourself walking toward Jesus, who is waiting with open, welcoming hands.

Place the burden in His hands and pray, either aloud or in the quiet of your heart, *This is Yours, Lord. Give me what I truly need for today.*

Take three slow, deep breaths, noticing how your shoulders relax as you shift from carrying it alone to carrying it with Jesus.

Stay for a moment and listen. Is there a gentle nudge, a small next step, or simply the reminder that Jesus is with you? Carry that peace into the rest of your day.

The Presence Pause

This practice is for those moments when life feels too crowded and your thoughts won't settle. Wherever you are – at your desk, stirring a pot on the stove or sitting in the car – let yourself pause. Take three slow, steady breaths, paying attention to the rise and fall of each inhale and exhale. Pray softly, *You are here, Lord. I am here with You.*

Open your senses one by one:

Notice one thing you can see.

Notice one thing you can hear.

Notice one thing you can feel against your skin.

Welcome a quiet thankfulness that reminds you God's presence is closer than your next breath.

Evening Renewal Reflection

Give yourself a few quiet minutes before sleep to let your soul unwind.

Take three slow, deep breaths, feeling the day settle.

Ask yourself:

Where did I notice Your presence today?

Where did I feel far from You?

What burden am I ready to place in Your hands tonight?

Offer a simple prayer of release, I rest in You, Lord. Hold what I cannot. Restore me as I sleep.

End by naming one or two small gifts from the day. A kind word, a moment of laughter, even the comfort of your bed and let gratitude close the day with peace.

Chapter 10
Living From the Vine

UP TO THIS point, we have been paying attention to the signals – the places in our bodies, our minds, and our souls that whisper (or shout) that something is off. We've noticed the weariness, the hurried pace, the constant pull to do more and be more. We've named our exhaustion and begun to imagine a different way.

God's desire for us is so much more than momentary relief or a spiritual "reset button." What Jesus offers is not simply a quick fix; it's a whole new way of being. This is where the journey takes another turn. From here, we move from noticing to rooting. From survival mode to abiding. From trying to keep ourselves together to letting Christ hold us together. Over the next chapters, we'll take this in a gentle, grace-filled order:

Rediscovering Values: getting clear about what matters most to you and Jesus.

Setting Gentle Intentions: prayerfully choosing the direction you are invited to move in.

Identity-Based Habits: letting small, meaningful habits grow out of your deepest identity in Christ so that you are formed from the inside out.

Bridging Belief and Behavior: reflecting regularly to notice where faith is shaping life.

Living in Holy Rhythm: incorporating these practices into a lifelong rhythm of grace, one that is sustainable and Spirit-led. Ultimately, a life of Breathing in Christ.

Abide in Me

Jesus' words in John 15:4-5 are among the most intimate invitations He ever offers:

"Abide in me as I abide in you. Just as the branch cannot bear fruit by itself unless it abides in the vine, neither can you unless you abide in me. I am the vine; you are the branches. Those who abide in me and I in them bear much fruit, because apart from me you can do nothing."

These words, spoken on the night before the cross, were deliberate and tender. They describe the very way spiritual life in Jesus happens. Life comes from Jesus alone. We are not lone trees, straining toward the sun by sheer willpower. We are branches grafted into a single, living Vine. Our existence, our nourishment, our growth – even our capacity to bear fruit – flows from Jesus.

This vision turns the world's wisdom upside down. Everywhere we turn, we're told to be self-sufficient, independent, and strong enough to "make something" of ourselves. Jesus offers an alternative way to live. You were created to grow in connection with Christ. Branches bear fruit only when they remain on the vine. That truth is humbling. It's also profoundly freeing. If faith has felt like a burden – if you've been weary from trying to hold everything together by yourself – then this image is a gift.

You are not asked to be the source of your own strength. You are invited to stay connected to the Vine. The Vine is a picture of shared life in union with Christ. The same sap that flows through the Vine flows through the branch. Jesus is the one who grows life within us. He is the Vine, drawing nourishment from God and pouring it into us. We are not left to manufacture growth on our own. Our invitation is simply this: to remain connected. To let the life of Jesus flow through us.

This is why abiding stands at the very heart of *Breathing in Christ*. Everything else – prayer, forgiveness, generosity, courage – flows out of this one connection. Fruit is the natural outcome of remaining close to Jesus and letting His life flow through you. To abide is to trust that Jesus is enough. It means resting in His sustaining presence, moment by moment. It means allowing His Word to shape your mind, His Spirit to direct your choices, and His love to fill you from the inside out.

Pause to Reflect: Take a deep breath. *Where in your life do you feel most connected to the Vine? Where do you feel disconnected?*

Why We Need a Trellis

Anyone who has walked through a vineyard knows that vines don't simply sprawl across the ground. They are trained to grow on a trellis. The trellis lifts the vine toward the light, allows space for air to flow, and creates room for fruit to ripen.

Our spiritual practices work in the same way. Breath prayer, Scripture meditation, Sabbath rest, community – they don't produce fruit on their own. They support the life that Jesus is already growing in us. Without a trellis, a vine runs along the ground. Fruit may still appear; however, it often rots before ripening. Disconnected from support, the branch is vulnerable and exhausted.

When we try to grow on our own – disconnected from spiritual rhythms, from community, from the Word of God – we can feel like those wild, ground-level branches. Vulnerable and exhausted. We may even still produce fruit. Often it comes with strain, burnout, or bitterness because we're trying to grow without support.

As you've learned by now, I've lived both ways. For a long season of my life, I was what you might call a "wild vine." My days were packed, my calendar full, and my prayer life mostly consisted of quick SOS requests when things went wrong. I believed in Jesus. I even worked for the church. I wasn't truly connected to Him in any daily, life-giving way. Honestly, I bore some fruit. Ministry happened, tasks got checked off, people were helped. Underneath, my soul was more vulnerable to discouragement, comparison, and self-doubt because I wasn't regularly drawing from the True Source.

It was Advent, quite a few years ago now, when I decided that year to pray with John 15. Slowly, every day, through the entire season leading to Christmas. At first, I thought it was a nice way to prepare for Christmas, a spiritual focus in the middle of a busy month. The longer I stayed with Jesus' words, "I am the vine; you are the branches. Remain in me." The more I realized where I was connected and where I wasn't.

Some parts of my life were branches securely growing on the trellis. Other parts of my life, okay *most parts of my life*, felt more like wild, ground-level vines. Tangled, weary, vulnerable. My prayer life was inconsistent. My pace was unsustainable. As I sat with the passage day after day, I began to sense that Jesus wasn't asking me to do more. He was inviting me to build support for what was already there, to let Him lift me toward the light.

I didn't get there all at once. Those first practices – breath prayer. Sabbath, gathering with others were simple, almost ordinary. Yet they created space for Jesus to grow something new in me. For the first time in a long time, I felt connected instead of alone. Jesus was producing something in me and through me that I could never have manufactured on my own. Underneath the support of those practices, I realized something else. The version of myself that had carried me this far, the part of me surviving on sheer determination and pushing through exhaustion, that self had done its job. It kept me afloat. And Jesus was showing me it wasn't the end of the story.

This is the moment in your *Breathing in Christ* journey to pause and notice the version of yourself that has carried you this far. That version kept you going. It helped you survive. You don't have to carry exhaustion forever.

Pause to Reflect: *What trellis practices are already part of your life? What supports might Jesus be inviting you to add?*

Survival isn't the goal anymore.

Every version of you had its reasons. These patterns grew out of longing, out of fear, out of the very human desire to be safe, to be loved, to be enough. Most of them worked, at least for a while. They kept you afloat when life felt overwhelming. You no longer have to keep living in survival mode. Now is the invitation to breathe deep and let Jesus reveal who you are becoming. This is the time to ask yourself, *Are these patterns still giving me life? Are they helping me bear fruit? Or are they keeping me small, exhausted, and hidden?*

The story you carry are gifts that brought you here. Now you are invited to move beyond survival patterns into a different way of living.

What if love was simply received as a gift?

What if being seen made space for your wholeness?

What if being fully known became the very place of safety?

This is your invitation. Let go of the lies that told you to hustle, prove, or hide. Breathe into the spacious life Jesus is already offering you. Love is a free gift. Being seen is a place for your wholeness. To be fully known in Christ is also to be fully safe. Right here, in this moment, Jesus promises: *You are enough. You are known. You are loved.* Begin receiving who you already are: beloved, chosen, and free.

From this place of belovedness, you are invited to look more closely at what truly matters – your deepest values. As you uncover what you most treasure in Christ, your life begins to take shape around God's love, growing into fruit that endures.

Chapter 11
Rediscovering Values

EVERY LIFE IS guided by values. Some we inherit. Some we absorb without realizing it. Some we choose with intention. Rediscovering your values invites Jesus back to your center. Values act like a compass. They orient you when you feel lost. They help you decide what to say *yes* to and when to let go. They reveal the difference between what drains you and what brings you life. Rediscovering your values is like uncovering the landmarks God has already planted within you – markers that point you toward a life that reflects Jesus' love.

Why Values Matter
Values are the why beneath the what.

Every decision you make – how you spend your morning, what you say "yes" to, what you decline – is connected to some deeply held belief about what matters most. Sometimes you're aware of it. Often your values are working quietly in the background, shaping your choices without you even realizing it. When you take a moment to recognize those values, you'll see just how deeply they shape everything around you. They are the compass points of your life, orienting you toward certain priorities and away from others.

Here's the reality: *if we don't name our values, the world will name them for us.*

And the world is very loud about what it thinks should matter: productivity, visibility, speed, efficiency, success, comparison. If we're not paying attention, we end up living lives that look full on the outside while feeling empty on the inside. Running faster, doing more, and wondering why we still feel restless. Rediscovering your faith values is a way of stepping back and saying, "I want my life to be shaped by Christ instead of the world's loudest and latest demands."

From a biblical perspective, values are more than personal preferences or lifestyle choices. When they are grounded in God's Word, they become reflections of God's own heart. The prophet Micah names this clearly. "What does the Lord require of you but to do justice, and to love kindness, and to walk humbly with your God?" (Micah 6:8). Jesus echoes this when He names the greatest commandments. "Love the Lord your God with all your heart, and with all your soul, and with all your mind… and love your neighbor as yourself" (Matthew 22:37-39). These passages teach us that the values God calls us to live by – love, justice, mercy, humility – are the very core of who we are as God's people. They form the DNA of God's Kingdom.

When Jesus said the greatest commandment is to love the Lord your God with all your heart, all your soul, and all your mind and to love your neighbor as yourself (Matthew 22:37–39), this means that Jesus cares how you spend your time. He cares about what your heart clings to and what you choose to prioritize. When love for God and love for neighbor become the wellspring of our decisions, our calendars, our commitments, even the words we speak start to reflect who we are in Christ rather than what the world demands. Living from Christ-shaped values rarely makes life suddenly easy or uncomplicated. Yet, it leads to a deeper sense of abiding. Instead of being pulled in a hundred directions, you find a steadier center of gravity – Jesus himself. Rediscovering faith values is one way we step into that steady center. It's a spiritual practice. A way of listening for what God is already planting in the soil of your life and making space for it to grow.

Jesus constantly reoriented His followers around Kingdom values. When people around Him were chasing status and recognition, Jesus knelt on the floor and washed His friends' dusty feet. When the culture admired strength and power, Jesus lifted up the meek and promised them the Kingdom. When religious leaders focused on rules and appearances, Jesus went straight to the heart offering mercy, healing, and welcome to those who had been pushed out.

Kingdom values are upside-down values: presence over productivity, compassion over competition, rest over relentless striving, truth over image, love over fear. They invite us to live in a way that may seem counter-intuitive at first. To slow down when everyone else is speeding up. To choose compassion even when it costs us. To make space for rest, trusting that our worth isn't tied to how much we accomplish. To tell the truth even when it might be easier to hide behind appearances. To let love, not fear, be the driving force behind our decisions.

This is what made Jesus' way so radical. He stopped for people others ignored. He welcomed children when His disciples wanted to send them away. He touched the sick, ate with outsiders, and saw worth in those the world had written off. When we live from Kingdom values, our lives start to look a little more like Jesus. Slower and gentler. Always rooted in what matters most. It might confuse people. It might even disrupt the status quo. It will also bear fruit that lasts. The kind that brings healing, hope, and light into the world.

The Birth of our Values

If values are the compass points of our lives, then it's worth asking: where do they come from? Why do some priorities feel so essential, so core to who we are, while others shift and change over time? The answers are layered and deeply personal. Our values are formed through a beautiful – and sometimes complicated – interplay between how God designed us, the stories we've lived so far, and the ongoing work of the Holy Spirit.

Before you drew your first breath, God saw you (Psalm 139:13-16). Before you knew your name, God spoke it. Scripture tells us that you are "God's handiwork, created in Christ Jesus for good works" (Ephesians 2:10).

Handiwork.

The Greek word here is *poiēma*, where we get the word poem. You are God's living, breathing poem.

Your value is not measured by how much you produce, how perfect you look, or how many people applaud. Your worth rests in the One who wrote you. Love is your divine blueprint. Love is your story of origin. Love is your birthright. Love is the soil you were planted in and the breath in your lungs.

Love is where everything begins.

This is why your soul longs for connection, why isolation feels so wrong, why rejection stings so deeply, and yes – why ASPCA commercials with the sad puppy eyes break your heart. You were created from love for love, which means the values that run deepest in you will always somehow point back to Jesus' love.

Some of those values feel like they have always been there. Part of the way you are wired. These are often connected to the way God uniquely created you: your temperament, your personality, even the spiritual gifts you've been given. Other values are shaped by your life experiences. What you've been taught, what you've celebrated, and sometimes even what you've survived. And then there is the ongoing work of the Holy Spirit. Always active, always forming and reforming us as we grow in Christ. The Spirit refines our values over time, gently pruning what no longer reflects God's heart and nurturing what is ready to flourish. Values, then, are both a gift and an invitation. God-given starting points continually shaped by the Spirit so that your life more closely reflects Christ's.

Living from the Person You Already Are

Every New Year, like clockwork, I find myself staring into the overstuffed abyss that is my closet. It always starts with the best of intentions. "This is the year," I tell myself. "This is the year I simplify. This is the year I create a pared-down closet with clothes I actually wear."

Less than twenty minutes in, I'm surrounded by piles of clothes and boxes I forgot existed, feeling more overwhelmed than organized. There are boots I haven't worn in five years but still keep, just in case. There's the "ten-pound wardrobe." You know the one. The clothes I don't fit into right now but just can't quite bring myself to give them away. Not yet. Surely this will be the year I lose those ten pounds and slip into the jeans I haven't worn since before the pandemic. Eventually I sit on the floor, surrounded by fabric and frustration, and it hits me: this isn't just a closet problem. This is a values problem. I've been dressing – not for who I am – but for some imaginary version of myself. A someday version. A "just in case" me. A me that's thinner, more put together, more acceptable.

I wonder how many of us live this way, holding on to versions of ourselves that we've outgrown or never really were. Trying to organize our lives by force when what we really need is to pause and ask: *What matters most now?*

What began as a tidy project became a soul check. Was I making decisions based on freedom or fear? Was I holding on to things out of identity or insecurity?

My closet had become aspirational more than actual. A visual representation of all the ways I felt I wasn't quite enough yet. Under the piles was a quiet invitation. "Live like the person you already are in Christ, not the one you think you have to become first."

Sometimes *Breathing in Christ* looks like keeping the boots I love (and will actually wear) and tossing the expectations that are just taking up space.

The Exhaustion of Earning

No one ever told me outright to "earn my worth." In fact, my family was full of love. There were bedtime stories and unhurried hugs. My parents celebrated who I was, not just what I did. And culture has a way of writing its own curriculum. Somewhere between childhood awards and adult expectations, I picked up a lie, "Your worth depends on how much you achieve." I believed that being loved meant being useful. That approval had to be earned. That showing up early, staying late, and faking it until I made it was just what good, faithful people did. Without meaning to, I carried that lie into my faith. I began to see God a bit like a kind supervisor. Watching, evaluating, quietly keeping score. I measured my faith the same way I measured everything else. Volunteer hours. Well-crafted prayers. A calendar crammed with ministry.

I didn't mean to perform my way into love. I was just doing what had always felt safe. Staying busy enough to avoid being seen too clearly. You can only outrun unworthiness for so long before something in you begins to break. I didn't realize how exhausted I was from trying to prove I was enough. Not just to other people but to God, too.

That's exactly where Jesus met me. In the pain.

I think of Peter in John 21. Not long after the resurrection, Jesus finds him on the beach. Breakfast is cooking over a charcoal fire; the same kind of fire Peter had stood near the night he denied Jesus three times.

The last time Peter stood by a fire, it wasn't love he offered. It was denial. Now, on this beach, Jesus asks him three times, "Simon son of John, do you love me?" One question for each denial. No lectures. No "I told you so." Just an invitation for Peter to speak the one thing shame had tried to silence, "Yes, Lord, you know that I love you."

Yes, Jesus forgives.

Yes, Jesus restores.

Yes, Jesus rewrites Peter's story.

And then He gives Peter a calling that grows out of love. "Feed my sheep." Peter – messy, impulsive, still healing – becomes the rock on which Jesus builds His church. This is what Jesus does. He meets us right in the middle of the mess, brings us back to the fire, and reignites our purpose.

Peter's story shows us what grace can do. Around that fire on the beach, Peter was reminded what his life was for. When Jesus meets us in the places where we've been living out of fear, striving, or self-protection, He offers us a chance to live differently, to move forward with a new center of gravity. This is where rediscovering our values becomes such a gift. When we pause long enough to notice what we have been living for, we begin to see where we are out of alignment. The closets full of old versions of ourselves, the overfull calendars that tell a story of proving rather than abiding. We get to ask the deeper questions:

What story has been shaping my life?

What am I holding onto that is weighing me down rather than setting me free?

What actually matters most to God and to me in this season?

Rediscovering your values gives you the chance to name what is truly important, as a way of saying, "Lord, I want my life to reflect what matters most to You." As you begin to name your faith values, you are putting language to the deepest longings God has already planted in you. Those words become a compass, helping you discern your yeses and your nos.

As with everything named in this book, this doesn't happen all at once. The Spirit works gently. This chapter gives you space to begin to look at your life like a mirror, to prayerfully notice what is shaping you, and to choose which values you want to nurture in this season. Allow it to be a slow, spacious conversation with Jesus. Write down what you notice. Pay attention to what stirs joy, conviction, or longing in you. Those are often clues to where the Spirit is at work. From there, move forward. One breath, one choice, one small, Spirit-led, rhythm at a time, as Jesus continues writing your story with His truth and grace.

Spiritual Practice: Naming Your Values in God's Presence

This is a moment to slow down and look closely at the life you're living right now. Your life already tells a story about what matters to you, what you love, and what you're longing for. These practices help you pay attention to that story. Step by step, you'll look at how you spend your time, where your energy goes, and what your habits reveal. You'll notice the patterns and ask, "What do these choices say about what I value right now?" Then, with prayer and gentle curiosity, you'll go deeper:

> What deeper desire is hiding beneath my habits, even the ones I'd like to change?
>
> Where is Jesus inviting me to grow or try something new?
>
> Which values feel ready to grow stronger, shift, or be let go?

Take your time. You can walk through these next steps all at once, or you can sit with them slowly over several days, weeks, or even months. Some values may come to you right away; others may take time to rise to the surface. The slower you go, the more space you give God to speak. By the end of this process, you'll have a short list – three to five words – that capture the values Jesus is calling you to live from in this season. These words become the foundation for your choices and invitations to keep *Breathing in Christ*.

Step One: Looking at Your Life Like a Mirror

Your actions often reveal what matters most to you. The way you spend your time, the habits that fill your days, and the choices you make – even the small, ordinary ones – serve as a mirror, reflecting the values you are actually living from in this season. Sometimes these values match the ones you hope to hold; other times, they may surprise you. Your calendar, your spending patterns, your energy levels, even the words you choose in conversation – all of these give clues to what your heart is prioritizing. Paying attention to these patterns can be one of the most powerful ways to discern what is truly shaping your life. Once you can see what you are living from, you can prayerfully consider whether those values are leading you toward the life

God desires for you or whether the Spirit might be inviting you to grow in a new direction. Take a slow inventory:

Your Calendar: What do you make time for, no matter what?

Your Bank Account: Where does your money naturally go?

Your Attention: What fills your thoughts when you're not distracted by a screen?

Your Energy: Who or what gets your best energy? Who gets only what's left over?

Your Yeses and Nos: Where do you say "yes" quickly? Where do you hesitate or avoid?

The answers are simply windows into what matters to you right now. They reveal where your time, energy, and attention are flowing. As you reflect, hold what you see with grace. The patterns help you notice where the Spirit is inviting you to grow.

Step Two: Ask What These Choices Reveal

Once you've written down where your time, energy, and attention have gone, pause and take a slow, compassionate look at what you see. Ask yourself:

What do my choices this week say about what I value right now?

Do these values reflect the life Jesus is inviting me to live?

Notice what story your life is telling. Maybe your calendar is packed from morning to night. That could reveal that you value productivity, responsibility, or caring for others, which are all good things. However, you might also notice a longing for rest or connection that is getting squeezed out.

Maybe you spend your evenings scrolling social media. That might show that you value fun, curiosity, or staying connected. If you end the night feeling restless or drained, it may be a sign that what you really long for is comfort or real connection; something your scrolling can't quite satisfy.

Maybe you say "yes" to nearly every request that comes your way. That can reflect a beautiful value of service, hospitality, or generosity. It might also show a longing to feel needed or loved and perhaps an invitation to trust that your worth doesn't depend on doing more.

And maybe there are choices you avoid altogether. Maybe you avoid conflict because you value peace. Or you put off decisions because you value caution or safety. Those choices are clues, too. Look for the patterns that show up again and again. Pay attention to what stirs your heart as you read over your list. The intention here is to grow your awareness. The more clearly you can see the values beneath your habits, the more freely you can choose whether to keep living from them or invite Jesus to reshape them.

Step Three: Find the Value Beneath the Surface

This is where the growth work moves from the surface to the soul. Every pattern in your life, even the ones you wish you could change, often points to something good underneath. Beneath your habits are holy longings:

> Busyness can reveal a value for meaning or purpose.
>
> Over-commitment might point to a longing to belong or to make a difference in the lives of others.
>
> Withdrawing from people may reflect a longing for peace or safety.
>
> Perfectionism could point to a longing for beauty, order, or harmony.
>
> Overworking might reveal a longing for security or to be seen as capable and valuable.

Seeing these habits through this lens allows you to respond with compassion rather than shame. Instead of scolding yourself for over-committing or staying up too late, you can ask, "What is my heart really reaching for?" This is where prayer becomes powerful. Sit quietly and invite Jesus into the moment: *Lord, help me see the good desire You have placed in me beneath this pattern. Show me what You are cultivating in the soil of my life.*

Wait for what comes. You might have a word or phrase rise up. You might picture something – a scene, a memory, an image. Or you might simply feel a gentle nudge or sense of knowing. Give yourself space to linger. You are doing holy work in letting the Spirit reframe your habits as clues to your deepest longings rather than problems to solve. What you discover may surprise you. You may find that the habit you most dislike in yourself is actually pointing to a God-given value that has been neglected or distorted. Instead of trying harder to "fix" the habit, you can look for ways to meet the longing in a way that keeps you connected to the Vine.

Step Four: Prayerfully Name Your Values

Now comes the part where you begin to put words to what you've discovered. After reflecting on your habits, your choices, and the longings underneath, take time to sit with Jesus and name the values you sense He is calling you to live from in this season.

Don't rush this. Find a quiet space, take a few deep breaths, and invite the Spirit to guide you: *Lord, show me what matters most right now. Reveal the values You want to grow in me. Help me name them with clarity and courage.*

As you listen, write down 3-5 words that feel alive for you. Words that give you a sense of joy, resonance, or even a holy ache. These words will become guides, helping you live with more intention in the weeks ahead. Here are some examples to help you imagine what these might look like:

Presence: Choosing to be here, fully attentive, instead of distracted or divided.

Compassion: Choosing to notice suffering and respond with love.

Courage: Choosing to do what is right, even when it is risky or hard.

Rest: Choosing rhythms that renew your soul and honor your limits.

Generosity: Choosing to live open-handedly, sharing what you have with others.

Integrity: Choosing to align your inner life with your outer actions.

Joy: Choosing to delight in God's good gifts, even the small, ordinary ones.

Your words may look different, and that is good. This is your conversation with Jesus. You might write words like curiosity, hope, belonging, peace, faithfulness, or trust. You might choose a phrase instead of a single word, like choose life or practice wonder. Allow this to be a prayerful experience, rather than a productivity exercise. You're not choosing words to impress anyone. You're naming the values that will help you stay connected to the Vine and live more fully into the life Christ is growing in you. If a word feels tender or challenging, don't dismiss it too quickly. Often, the value that stirs something deep in us is the very one God is inviting us to embrace. When you have your list, read it back to Jesus and sit with how it feels. Do these words bring you a sense of peace? Do they stretch you toward growth in a life-giving way?

Step Five: Keep Your Values Where You Can See Them

Once you've prayerfully named your values, give them a visible place in your life. These words are intended to keep you grounded and intentional as you move through your days. Write them somewhere you will notice them often:

In your journal, where you can revisit them during prayer or reflection.

On a note card by your bed or taped to your bathroom mirror, so they are the first words you see in the morning.

As a screensaver or background on your phone, so you're reminded of them throughout the day.

The more you see your faith values, the more you'll find yourself living from them. Read them often. Pray over them. Ask Jesus to help you let these values shape your choices – the way you spend your time, how you respond to interruptions, what you say *yes* to, and what you release. These words become companions, guiding the pace of your life and the direction of your energy. They will remind you Whose you are and who you are becoming in Christ.

Chapter 12
Setting Gentle Intentions: Planting the Seeds

"Commit your work to the Lord, and your plans will be established." (Proverbs 16:3)

ONCE YOU'VE NAMED what matters most – your Christ-shaped faith values – the natural question becomes, "Now what?" How do you take those values from words on a page and begin living them in real time? It's one thing to circle a word on a list or jot it down in your journal. It's another to let that value show up in how you speak, how you make decisions, how you spend your time, and even how you handle challenges. Values on paper are like seeds in a packet – full of life and potential – not yet growing. They need to be planted, nurtured, and tended if they're going to bear fruit in your daily life. Values are the *why* behind your life. They are the compass pointing you toward the direction God is calling you to go. A compass alone won't get you anywhere. You could stand in the middle of the forest, gripping it in your hand all day long, marveling at how faithfully the needle points north, and still never move an inch closer to where you need to be. This is where intention-setting comes in.

If values are the compass, intentions are the steps you take in the direction the compass points. Intentions are where the inner *why* of your life meets the outer *how* of your everyday living. They translate what you care about most into how you speak, how you respond, how you spend your time, and how you show up for the people around you. Intentions are the bridge between belief and action, between the convictions you carry in your heart and the habits that create your days.

Intentions are different from resolutions. Resolutions demand perfection and leave little room for grace. Intentions, on the other hand, are about direction. Gentle, Spirit-led movements of the heart that orient you toward the life you long to live in Christ. They're the choices to put one foot in front of the other. Knowing where north is and taking steps in that direction.

This is where spiritual practices and everyday life come together. Values are a beautiful starting point. They give us a vision for what matters most. They can feel distant if we leave them simply as ideas on a page. Intentions help bring those values close. They give them shape in real life, in the small, ordinary moments where faith is lived out. Intentions are what carry our values into the dinner table conversations, the way we respond to interruptions, the decisions we make when no one else sees, even the way we face challenges. Your values might reveal that generosity matters to you. Setting an intention is what helps generosity find its way into your budget, your schedule, and your relationships. Your values may remind you that rest is sacred. Intention is what gently protects space for Sabbath, even when the to-do list is long.

Intentions invite us to move from simply admiring the compass to actually moving in its direction. Slowly, steadily, with grace. When intentions are centered in Christ, they do more than keep us moving. They help us breathe in Christ.

Paul says it beautifully in Philippians 4:4-9. He begins by painting a picture of the heart's posture: rejoicing always, choosing gentleness, praying about everything, and practicing gratitude. These are values that shape our inner life. Paul doesn't stop here. He closes with this gentle and clear invitation: *Keep putting into practice all you learned and received from me – everything you heard from me and saw me doing. Then the God of peace will be with you.*

In other words, values are meant to be lived. It's one thing to value gentleness; it's another to respond with a calm voice to your child when you're running late and every part of you feels impatient. It's one thing to say prayer matters; it's another to pause mid-afternoon, take a deep breath, and actually hand your anxiety to Jesus. Paul understood that values are meant to move from the heart into our everyday lives, shaping our words, our tone, our calendars, even the way we spend our money. This is where values become visible, embodied in the way we treat the person standing right in front of us.

This is often where we find our roadblocks. Holding a beautifully clear compass, yet staying in place. It might feel as though having clarity about our values is enough. Thinking that once we've named what matters, everything else will fall into place.

Life has a way of filling up with noise, demands, and distractions. Competing priorities will always pull at our attention. When we take even one small, intentional step in the direction Jesus is leading, our beliefs begin to take shape as daily rhythms. This is what intentions are for. They give shape and direction to what we say matters most.

A value like peace is a beautiful desire, and it stays only as an idea until we choose how to live into it. Intentions make our values tangible. An intention might sound like: "As someone who wants to experience more peace, every morning I will begin the day with Jesus before I look at my phone." That one choice turns peace from an aspiration into something that actually shows up in our mornings, our schedule, and even in the tone we carry into the day.

When our intentions are shaped by the Spirit and rooted in Christ's love, they are more than self-improvement plans. They become grace-filled invitations for Jesus to form us from the inside out. Even when life feels messy or unpredictable, intentions help us keep moving toward Jesus. They remind us that growth is less about striving and more about abiding, less about doing more and more about staying connected to the Vine.

As we move into this next part of the *Breathing in Christ journey*, we'll take the values you've prayerfully named and turn them into Christ-centered intentions. This is where your *why* begins to take shape as a *how*. Where what matters most to you starts becoming part of your daily life. We'll also look at how to incorporate these intentions into your everyday routines so they actually shape your *yes*es and *no*s.

Planting Your Values in the Soil of Daily Life

This is the planting stage of the journey where the seeds of your values are pressed gently into the soil of everyday life. Intentions are like tender shoots. They need time, light, and care to grow strong. We won't rush this process. Instead, we'll ask Jesus to help us see what step He's inviting us to take next.

Think of this as holy experimentation. You get to try small, Spirit-led practices and see how they shape your inner life and outer actions. Even one or two simple intentions can begin to transform the way you move through your day. Some will stick and grow deep roots. Others you may lay aside and try again later. Over time, they create new rhythms that keep you close to the Vine.

The truth is, two people can do the very same thing: serve at a soup kitchen, lead a Bible study, bring a meal to a neighbor. On the outside, it all looks identical. On the inside? One person may be acting out of love for Jesus and a genuine desire to serve. The other may be acting out of fear of letting someone down, or from a need to feel important, or from the hope that others will notice. Honestly, most of us have probably experienced both sides of that coin. It's humbling when we realize that even our *good* can sometimes be tangled up with self-serving motives. This is precisely why intention matters. The heart behind the action shapes the fruit it produces. A *yes* rooted in love and humility is not the same as a *yes* driven by fear or pride. When we notice our intentions with a gentle, curious heart, we make room for the Spirit to do what only the Spirit can do: shape our motives, soften our hearts, and draw us closer to Jesus.

Intentions vs. Goals

Before we go any further, I want to talk about the difference between intentions and goals, and why this distinction matters so much for a life of *Breathing in Christ*. Intentions are simply statements of direction. They are the bridge between the values we've named and the habits we will eventually practice. Think of them like seeds. Small, simple, sometimes barely visible, yet full of potential for growth.

While goals have their place, they are outcome focused. They sound like: "I want to lose 10 pounds." "I want to read the Bible in a year." "I want to save $5,000." Goals can be helpful because they give you something to aim for and measure. They point you toward a finish line. And when you cross that finish line, it can feel satisfying to check the box and celebrate. Intentions are different. They are process focused. They are about how you live while you are on the journey. Intentions may sound more like: "I intend to honor my body with movement." "I intend to eat in a way that fuels me." "I intend to begin my mornings with Jesus."

Do you hear the difference? Goals measure success in check boxes and streaks; intentions measure success in presence and direction. Goals can create pressure and even shame when you miss a day or slip up. Intentions invite you back, again and again, no matter how many times you wander. An intention shapes the way you run the race, not just whether you cross the finish line. It's less about arriving and more about staying connected to Jesus along the way. Intentions keep guiding you even as life changes. A goal might end once it's accomplished, an intention continues to form who you are becoming in Christ. For example, you might set a goal to pray every day for a month. That's a great goal! However, if the deeper intention is only to check prayer off your to-do list, the practice might start to feel rushed or empty. If the intention is "I will open my heart to Jesus and listen for His voice," the practice becomes a living encounter. Something that nourishes you well beyond the month.

Intentions breathe life into goals. They give goals their soul. They turn what could be project of self-improvement into a rhythm that keeps drawing you back to the Vine, shaping who you are day by day, and helping you live more deeply connected to Jesus. Intentions are more like prayers than promises. A promise says, *I will do this, no matter what.* A prayer says, *Lord, this is the desire of my heart. Help me live into this with You.* Intentions feel like open hands rather than clenched fists. They name the direction you long to move toward, while leaving space for grace when you fall, rest, or need to begin again. When you hold your intentions as prayers, they become conversations with Jesus rather than measurements and free us from all-or-nothing thinking. They keep us attuned to the One who is doing the deeper work within us.

Intentions as an Act of Grace

Setting an intention is choosing to participate in the life of the Vine. To welcome the work Jesus is already doing and let His life shape yours. Think of intentions as a holy *yes*. When you set an intention, you are saying *yes* to God's ongoing work in you. You are saying *yes* to letting Jesus grow something new, even if it begins small. You are saying *yes* to being shaped by love rather than fear, by grace rather than striving. Intentions are an open-handed prayer: *"Lord, this is the direction I long to move. Teach me to walk with You here."* Each intention you set is planting a seed, trusting that the Gardener will tend to it. Watering, pruning, providing light at just the right time. Though the growth is hidden beneath the surface at first, holy work is happening. The roots go down first. The hidden work of grace prepares the way for visible fruit. This is why intentions are acts of grace. They release us from the pressure to control the outcome and invite us into a posture of trust. We are invited to plant and to be present. God is the faithful Gardener who brings the harvest.

Abiding With Purpose: Setting Holy Intentions

You've named your faith values. Now comes the fun part: turning those values into intentions that guide your everyday life. You are now taking your values off the shelf, dusting them off, and inviting them into the kitchen where real life happens. I am going to walk you through a simple and powerful process for setting Christ-centered intentions. The process has five steps. They're simple. Don't rush them. Each one invites you to slow down and engage both your mind and your spirit, so your intentions are living commitments that shape the way you show up in the world.

Step One: Begin in Prayer

Before you do anything else, take a moment to pause and pray. Quiet your mind, slow your breathing, and invite the Spirit to guide you. You might pray something as simple as: *Jesus, You are the true Vine. Show me where You are inviting me to grow in this season. Help me choose the value that will draw me closer to You and align my life with Your love.* Sit for a moment in silence and let this prayer settle you.

Step Two: Look Back at Your Values

Pull out the list of three to five values you prayerfully named in the last chapter. Read them slowly – maybe even aloud – and notice what stirs as you see them on the page.

Which value feels most tender right now? Pay attention to the one that catches your breath or stirs something deep, maybe even a little ache or longing. Tenderness often points to an area of growth or healing that is ready for Jesus.

Which value feels most out of alignment with the way I'm living these days? Notice where the Spirit may be inviting you to come back into holy rhythm. The places that feel out of step can often be the very places where Jesus wants to meet you with grace.

Where do I sense Jesus' invitation to grow deeper? Sometimes this comes as a gentle nudge, a value that draws your attention again and again. Sometimes it feels like conviction, a loving call to re-center your life around what matters most.

Sometimes one value will rise to the surface right away. Other times, it takes a little sitting still before you sense where Jesus is nudging you.

Step Three: Choose Just One for This Season

You may have several values that are deeply important to you. Trying to act on all of them at once can feel overwhelming and lead to discouragement. Instead, choose one to begin with just for this season.

If your value is rest, your intention might sound like: *I intend to create space for Sabbath moments each week.*

If your value is presence, your intention might sound like: *I intend to be fully present with the people right in front of me.*

If your value is generosity, your intention might sound like: *I intend to live openhandedly, trusting God to supply what I need.*

When you choose one value, you make it possible to pay attention to it and practice it in small, tangible ways. Example:

Value: Presence

Intention: "I will put my phone down during dinner and really listen to the people at my table."

See how clear and doable that is? You can tell whether you're living it. And it's grace filled. Intentions like this simply invite you to pay attention. Each time you put your phone down at dinner, you're choosing presence. Each time you forget and catch yourself scrolling, you're given another chance to gently realign with what matters most. This is the beauty of intentions. They always leave room to begin again. When you approach intentions this way, they become a source of freedom rather than pressure. They give you clarity about how you want to show up in the world – at the dinner table, in your workplace, with your kids or friends – and they keep pointing you back to Jesus when the noise of life pulls you away.

A woman in my coaching group recently shared that her value was *peace*. Her first draft intention was, "I want to feel less stressed." We worked together to shape it into, *I choose to begin each workday with five minutes of breath prayer before opening my email.* That redirect gave her a practical starting point for cultivating peace every single morning.

Once you've chosen the value you want to focus on and shaped it into an intention, pause for a moment and offer it back to God. You might pray: *"Lord, I place this intention in Your hands. Grow it in me through Your Spirit and let it bear fruit that reflects Your heart."* This simple act turns your intention into a prayer. Something alive and Spirit-led, rather than just another line on a to-do list.

Step Four: Make it Specific and Spacious

Once you've chosen your value and shaped it into an intention, take a moment to make sure it's clear enough to guide you – and spacious enough to leave room for grace. Intentions work best when they give you a direction to walk in, rather than a rigid rule to follow. If your intention feels too strict, it may create pressure instead of freedom. If it's too vague, it might not actually change how you live. The sweet spot is somewhere in between, a gentle container that holds your value and helps it grow. For example: Instead of, "I will never look at my phone after 9 p.m." try "I intend to wind down in the evening with less screen time so my soul can rest."

Hear the difference? The second statement is still clear. It gives you a way to live into your value and it leaves space for real life. There will be nights when you stay up late catching up with a friend or FaceTiming your grandkids and that's okay. The goal is to create space for rest, not to punish yourself when life doesn't go exactly as planned.

Here's another example. Instead of "I will journal for 30 minutes every morning," try "I intend to begin my mornings by listening for God's voice, whether that's through a few minutes of journaling, reading Scripture, or simply sitting with Jesus in silence." This version gives your intention room to flex with your schedule and your energy levels, while still keeping you oriented toward the value of being present with God.

The woman in my coaching group who recently named peace as one of her core values, as we talked about what that might look like as an intention, her first thought was, *"I just want to feel less stressed."* That was a good place to start. It named her desire but it didn't yet give her a way to practice peace in her daily life. Together, we shaped it into something more specific and doable, *"I choose to begin each workday with five minutes of breath prayer before opening my email."* That one simple shift gave her a concrete starting point for cultivating peace every single morning. It turned her value into something she could live out and gave her a practice to return to whenever her day started to spiral.

A trellis doesn't force a vine into a perfect shape. It simply gives it support so it can grow upward and flourish. Your intention is like that trellis. It holds you gently, giving your value structure without squeezing out joy or spontaneity.

Once you've shaped your intention, say it out loud. *Does it feel life-giving? Does it make you breathe a little deeper?* If so, you're on the right track.

Step Five: Imagine What It Might Feel Like

Once you've named your intention, give yourself a moment to really picture it. Close your eyes and imagine what your life might feel like if you lived from this intention for a week, a month, a year. Ask yourself:

> How would I feel at the end of the day? More present? More rested?
>
> What might change about my mornings, my workdays, or my conversations?
>
> How might others experience me differently: my partner, my kids, my coworkers, the barista who sees me every Wednesday?

Allow yourself to feel what it would actually be like to live in alignment with this value. This kind of holy imagination helps your heart and body catch up with what your spirit already knows is possible.

Stack It Onto Something You Already Do

Once you can see it in your mind, the next step is to give your intention a place to live in your actual day. One of the simplest ways to do this is through habit stacking – linking your new intention to something you already do without thinking about it.

Here's how it works: take something that's already a daily rhythm and "stack" your new practice right on top of it. Examples:

> Value: Presence → After you pour your morning coffee, take three deep breaths and thank God for a new day before looking at your phone.
>
> Value: Prayer → After brushing your teeth at night, sit on the edge of the bed and pray a short prayer of gratitude.
>
> Value: Rest → After you close your laptop at the end of the day, step outside and breathe in the evening air before rushing into dinner prep or errands.
>
> Value: Generosity → After receiving your paycheck, pause for a moment and thank Jesus for His abundance before you pay bills or make purchases.

Habit stacking takes the guesswork out of when to practice your intention. Instead of leaving it to chance, you connect your new practice to something that's already part of your daily rhythm: pouring your coffee, brushing your teeth, shutting down your laptop. This simple pairing makes your new intention easier to remember and gives it a natural place to live in your day. This makes the new rhythm almost effortless, muscle memory for your soul. We'll explore this idea more deeply in the next chapter, looking at practical ways to "stack" holy habits into the flow of your ordinary routines so they can take root and grow.

Finally, pause and offer your intention to God. As a holy exchange, take a deep breath, hold your intention in your heart, and imagine placing it gently into Jesus' hands. You might pray, *Holy Spirit, remind me of this intention when I need it most. Lead me to choose in a way that reflects Your love and keep growing Your life within me.* When you pray this way, your intention moves from being just a good idea to becoming a conversation with Jesus. It becomes a living, grace-filled practice, one that supports a life of *Breathing in Christ*. This is the beauty of intentions shaped in God's presence. They draw you deeper into the Vine, where your doing flows out of your being. Each time you remember and return to your intention, you are abiding, letting Christ's life flow through you. Small, ordinary steps become holy ground when they are taken with Jesus.

Chapter 13
Discovering a Life of Breathing In Christ

STOP FOR JUST a moment and celebrate your journey so far! You've named
the values that matter most and allowed them to be reshaped into Christ-centered
intentions. These are your holy *yeses.* Prayerful commitments that express how
you long to abide with Jesus. Intentions, as powerful as they are, still need a place
to land. They need somewhere to live, a rhythm that carries them into the ordinary
moments of your days. Without that rhythm, even the clearest intentions risk fading
into the background as good ideas rather than becoming the life you're actually
living. This is where habits play a vital role.

Habits make space for your values to become visible, embodied, and fruitful in
everyday life. They are your trellis. Small, repeated choices that give your intentions
a place to take root and grow. Habits are like the steady breaths of your spiritual life.
Just as each inhale and exhale keeps your body alive, these small, repeated rhythms
keep your soul nourished and connected to Christ.

Let's explore how to turn your intentions into daily and weekly rhythms that are
realistic, life-giving, and sustainable. Ultimately, this is what *Breathing in Christ*
looks like. Allowing the life of Jesus to flow into every moment, until even the
ordinary rhythms of your day become holy ground.

How Habits Are Formed

Every day is filled with hundreds, even thousands, of small choices. Most of them
we barely notice. Which sock to put on first. Whether to grab the red mug or the blue
one. What route to take to work. On their own, these choices may feel insignificant.
Yet together, they create the patterns and rhythms that form our lives. It isn't just
our choices that are shaping us. We are always being formed. By the creation around
us. By the culture we live in. By the environment that holds us. The advertising
we scroll past. The conversations we overhear. The pace of the world's demands.
All of these influence who we are becoming. Every moment carries its own kind of

shaping power. If we're always being formed by something, then the invitation is to be formed intentionally. To allow Christ's love and presence to guide the shaping of our days, so that our lives grow in alignment with Him rather than by default to everything else.

If everything around us is forming us, then habits are one of the most powerful ways we participate in that formation. A habit is simply a choice repeated often enough that it becomes automatic, shaping us almost without effort. Think about brushing your teeth. You don't debate it every morning. You simply brush your teeth without even thinking about it. That's the hidden gift of habits. They save you from decision fatigue, freeing up mental energy and emotional bandwidth for the bigger, deeper things in life. Charles Duhigg, in *The Power of Habit*, explains that habits usually follow a three-step pattern:

1. *Cue* - Something signals your brain to begin a behavior.

2. *Routine* - The action or behavior itself.

3. *Reward* - The benefit your brain associates with the behavior, which motivates you to repeat it.

For example, maybe you keep your Bible on your pillow. That's your *cue*. When you see it at night, you open it and read. That's the routine. The sense of peace you feel as you fall asleep grounded in God's Word becomes the *reward*. Over time, your brain begins to anticipate that reward, making the behavior more automatic. Spiritually, this is beautiful news. It means that we can intentionally shape our lives so that small choices keep drawing us back to the Vine without constant effort or willpower.

The Power of Small Habits

Most of us long for change, so we reach for it in one giant leap. We decide we'll completely overhaul our diet, read the Bible in a year, wake up at 5 a.m. for prayer, and keep a spotless house – all at once. The problem is that giant leaps often leave us exhausted. What starts as inspiration quickly turns into burnout.

Jesus offered a different picture. He compared the Kingdom of God to a mustard seed so small it could rest on the tip of your finger, yet capable of growing into something expansive and strong (Matthew 13:31-32). Habits work the same way. They begin small, almost laughably small. Given time, they take root and grow into something that shapes you deeply. Think of your habits as seeds planted in the soil of your daily life. They may not look like much at first. One minute of prayer before you check your phone. Adding one nourishing meal into your week. Pausing for a single deep breath before you respond in a tense conversation. These small practices lower the barrier to entry, making them simple enough to repeat. And repetition is what helps the roots grow strong.

God has always formed humanity through patterns and rhythms. In the Old Testament, Israel was given Sabbath days, annual festivals, and daily prayers. These were holy rhythms that taught people to remember who they were and Whose they were. The rhythm itself became a teacher. The Sabbath taught them to trust God with both their work and their rest. The festivals helped them celebrate God's faithfulness. Daily prayers turned their hearts toward God again and again. Over time, these repeated patterns formed their identity and shaped how they lived in the world.

Habits work like that trail through the woods. The first time you walk it, you push through tangled branches and tall grass. The second time, it's a little easier. Keep walking, and soon you've cleared a path you can follow without thinking. Habits carve out those pathways in your brain and soul. With each repetition, an intentional choice becomes less effortful, more natural, until it feels like second nature. Small, Christ-centered habits are the daily breaths – the tiny seeds – shaping you from the inside out.

My coach has a saying I love. *"What got you here, will not get you there."* The habits that carried you this far may not be the same ones that will lead you into the life Jesus is inviting you to now. Some habits were survival patterns. Good for a season. Not meant to last forever. Others were stepping stones, preparing you for what comes next. The way forward is rarely through massive, unsustainable leaps.

The invitation is to start small. Aim for what one of my mentors calls a *B-habit,* something simple enough to do on an ordinary day, even on a tired day. These small steps build momentum. Like pennies dropped into a jar, each tiny choice accumulates until one day you look back and realize how much has changed.

Researchers like BJ Fogg and James Clear describe this as the power of compounding. Every small action is a vote for the person you are becoming. Spiritually, every Christ-centered choice you make is a way of closing the gap between who you already are in Christ and how you actually live day by day.

Habit Stacking: Making Change Simple

One of the simplest ways to create new rhythms is through what behavioral scientists call *habit stacking* – attaching a new practice to something you already do without thinking. James Clear, in *Atomic Habits*, explains that our brains love predictability. When we link a new action to a well-established one, we lower the friction. The established habit acts like a trigger, reminding us to begin again.

Think about your mornings. You already pour the coffee, brush your teeth, or open your laptop. Those moments are like hooks, waiting for something holy to hang on them. Instead of forcing an entirely new routine, you borrow the strength of one that already exists.

> After you pour your morning coffee, take one slow, intentional breath and pray, "Lord, I receive this day from You."
>
> After you brush your teeth at night, open your Bible and read a single verse.
>
> When you sit down at your desk, offer a one-line prayer. "Jesus, guide my work today."

At first, these small shifts might feel clunky, almost like writing with your non-dominant hand. That's normal. Your brain is still connecting the dots, laying down fresh neural pathways. Each time you repeat the stack, the connection grows stronger. Eventually, what once felt awkward becomes as natural as flipping on a light switch when you enter a room.

The beauty of habit stacking is how ordinary it feels. You're not carving out a brand-new hour for prayer or reorganizing your whole life. You're weaving Christ's presence into your actual day. One by one, these stacked habits form a trellis lifting your attention, your energy, and your spirit toward the Vine. Before long, they are no longer just "practices" you do; they become the way you breathe.

One of my favorite ways to practice habit stacking is while brushing my teeth. As someone who spends a lot of time writing and speaking, I know just how desperately I need Jesus in my words. Every morning as I scrub away, I pray: "Lord, please scrub my words, too. Purify the things I think, say, and write so they bring love and not harm. And Lord, if there's any leftover gunk, scrub it out before it sneaks into a sermon, a meeting, or, heaven forbid, a reply-all email."

Who knew minty toothpaste could become a brief morning liturgy? Honestly, it works for me. My toothbrush is a daily reminder that words can either build people up or tear them down, and I need Jesus in the mix if I want mine to do the first.

The same thing happens in the shower. While the water is rinsing away yesterday's grime, I remember my baptism. I picture Jesus washing off the junk I've picked up, the unhelpful thoughts, the sharp words I wish I hadn't said, the exhaustion that clings like soap scum. By the time I am dried off, I feel lighter. Still me, still flawed, still in need of grace – while also freshly reminded that Jesus makes all things new – even me. Taking the things we already do – brushing, scrubbing, rinsing – allowing them to become reminders that we're loved, cleansed, and being shaped by Christ makes the habit stacking holy and powerful.

Reflection & Practice

Where in your daily routine might you pause to remember Jesus' presence? Think about the "ordinary" things: brushing your teeth, pouring coffee, buckling a seat belt, or walking the dog.

What words, thoughts, or actions in your life could use a little holy scrubbing? How might you invite Jesus to cleanse or re-center you in those moments?

When do you feel most weighed down by yesterday's junk? Could a shower, hand-washing, or even washing the dishes become a time to remember your baptism and God's promise of renewal?

What's one small, practical way you could stack prayer onto a habit you already have? For example:

> Before you unlock your phone, offer a one-line prayer, "Guide my attention, Lord."
>
> As you wait for the microwave, pray for someone on your heart.
>
> When you turn off the lights at night, thank God for one gift from the day.

Which habit would you like to try this week? How might you keep it simple enough to actually practice, even on your most tired days?

Living Your Values, One Habit at a Time

Some years ago, I sat down with a mentor who asked me a question I still hear in my heart: *Marsha, if I followed you around for a week, what would I learn about what you value most?* I wanted to throw up. If someone had shadowed me then, they probably would have seen how committed I was to answering emails, meeting deadlines, exceeding expectations and keeping the wheels of ministry turning. Would they have seen my deepest values? I wasn't so sure. It was one thing to say what I valued. It was another thing to live them out in small, ordinary ways. The question isn't whether we have habits. It's whether those habits reflect the values we hold most dear in Christ. It's time now to let your values move from aspiration to action, from words to rhythms, from intention to lived reality.

Here's the beautiful thing about habits: they're simply small choices we repeat until they become part of us. They're the everyday rhythms that tell the truth about what matters most. And here's the grace. You don't have to overhaul your whole life in one giant leap. Transformation usually grows in seed-sized steps. For example,

If your value is, *rest,* your habit might be lighting a candle and pausing for five minutes of quiet before bed, letting your body know the day is done. If your value is being truly *present*, your habit might be turning your phone face down during dinner so your eyes and attention belong to the people at your table. Take *compassion* as your value. Your habit might be saying a silent prayer each time you notice someone who looks tired, burdened, or overlooked. Or maybe the value is *generosity.* Your habit might be choosing one small way each week to share, whether that's a meal, a ride, or a listening ear.

None of these require hours of your day or superhuman discipline. They're gentle, doable, repeatable. Repeated over time, they form a pattern – a trellis – that supports the kind of life you long to live in Christ.

When we shape habits from our values, we stop living reactively, as though the loudest demand of the moment always gets the last word. Instead, our lives breathe more deeply in Christ. This is how faith takes shape in the everyday: in the dishes, the inbox, the commutes, the conversations. One choice at a time, one rhythm at a time, one holy breath at a time.

Spiritual Practice: Writing a Simple Rule of Life

One powerful way to live into your intentions is to create what Christians through the centuries have called a *Rule of Life.* At first, the word "rule" might sound rigid or heavy; however, the root word *regula* actually means "trellis." Think of the wooden frame that supports a grapevine or climbing rose. The trellis doesn't control the plant; it simply holds it in place so it can grow tall, steady, and fruitful.

A Rule of Life works the same way. It gives your values and intentions something to lean on so they don't remain abstract ideas. Instead, they begin to bear fruit in your everyday rhythms. A Rule of Life creates a structure that helps you flourish. A framework that keeps you rooted in Christ, even when life gets noisy or unpredictable. Here's how you can begin writing your own:

Step 1 - Write Your Core Value
Choose one value that feels especially important in this season.

Example: Being present.

Step 2 - Write Your Intention
Shape that value into a guiding intention for daily living.

Example: I intend to practice being fully present in my relationships.

Step 3 - Name 1 or 2 Simple Practices
Think of practices as the supports on your trellis. Small, repeatable actions that help your intention take root. Keep them simple and realistic.

Example: Put away my phone during dinner. Begin conversations with eye contact and a deep breath. Notice how specific these are. You can actually tell whether you're living them. And they're gentle enough to feel like invitations instead of burdens.

Think of your Rule of Life like a recipe card you keep tucked in your kitchen. It doesn't need to be long or complicated. A few clear ingredients – your value, your intention, your simple practices – are enough to guide you. Or picture it like setting up a trellis in your garden. The trellis doesn't force the plant to grow. It creates the right conditions for growth. In the same way, your Rule of Life helps your soul grow in the direction of Jesus' love.

Your Rule of Life is allowed to evolve. You may adjust it as your season of life changes or as the Spirit nudges you toward new rhythms. What matters is that you've created a gentle structure to help your values become visible in the way you live, breathe, and move through the world.

The Tug-of-War Between Urgent and Important

One of the sneakiest saboteurs of intention is the pull of other people's expectations. Often disguised as loyalty, helpfulness, or being a "team player," let's be honest: it feels good to be dependable, capable, the one others can always count on. Until suddenly, you realize you've been showing up to everyone else's life – and missing your own.

It can feel like living in the middle of a "should storm." You should work harder and rest more. You should say "yes" to every opportunity and also have impeccable boundaries. You should be stylish, frugal, spiritual, eco-conscious, wildly successful, and perfectly relaxed. Trying to carry all those shoulds is like packing for every possible climate in one suitcase. You end up lugging around too much, and none of it actually fits the trip you're on.

The way through? Know your *yes*. Name your faith-shaped values and let them set the tone for your decisions. Say "no" to some good things so you can say "yes" to the *right* things. Even Jesus did so without apology because He was living from God's rhythm.

One practice that has saved me again and again is what I call *the pause*. That small space between a request and your response. It might sound like, "Let me think about it." Or, "Can I get back to you by Friday?" For me, it often looks like ignoring the buzzing phone until I'm centered enough to respond with clarity rather than guilt. That pause is where you can breathe, pray, and remember what matters most before you commit.

It also helps to keep a "sanity squad" of friends or mentors who love you enough to notice when you're drowning in *yeses* you didn't mean to give. My people know the cue: three simple words, breathe in Christ. Those words pull me back from overdrive into God's rhythm.

Then there's the short list. Every morning at 8:00 a.m., my calendar pings me: intention setting. I jot down two or three things that matter most that day. Not ten. Not twenty. Just two or three. That list becomes my compass. So, when the unexpected email or "quick favor" comes, I can weigh it against the commitments I've already named with God. Some things wait. Some things get released. And my *yeses* come from clarity.

Does this mean you'll nail it every week? Heck no. Some weeks you'll feel grounded, aligned, even energized. Other weeks you'll forget what your values are, eat cereal for dinner, and run on empty fumes. That's okay. This was never about becoming a spiritual superhero. It's about becoming yourself – on purpose – with grace leading the way.

Which brings us back to why you picked up this book in the first place. Maybe you were exhausted. Maybe your days felt full but your spirit felt empty. Maybe you were longing for a deeper way of living with Jesus. Take a breath and look back at the path we've walked together. Each step has built on the last, creating a graceful arc of growth:

> Values – the why behind your life. What matters most, rooted in Jesus.
>
> Intentions – the how. The guiding principles that turn values into daily direction.
>
> Habits – the what you do, repeated until it becomes second nature.
>
> Rhythms – the flow of grace that takes shape through those habits, forming a holy pattern for living.
>
> Rule of Life – the trellis that supports it all, giving structure and stability so you can keep growing in Christ.

This is the framework of *Breathing in Christ*. A way of moving from exhaustion to alignment, from striving to abiding, from trying harder to receiving grace in the everyday. Before you close this book, I want to give you a way to carry its heart with you into tomorrow and the next season and the one after that.

Revisit your values and intentions often. Each season of life brings new challenges and new opportunities. Take time, maybe at the start of each quarter, or with each change of season, to prayerfully look at your values again. *What still feels true? What feels tender? Where is God inviting you to grow deeper?*

If this matters to you, treat it like it matters. Put it on your calendar. Block an hour on a Sunday afternoon or the first day of spring. Set a reminder in your phone. Write yourself a note and stick it on the fridge. Whatever will help you remember, do it. This isn't busywork. This is soul work. Just like we schedule doctor's visits, team meetings, or coffee with a friend, we can schedule time with Jesus to check in on what's shaping our lives. Think of it as an appointment with your deepest self and with Jesus. By writing it down or setting a notification, you're saying *this is important enough to show up for.* Every time you revisit your values and intentions, you give the Spirit space to refresh what's growing in you.

See your daily habits as seeds of resurrection. Even the smallest practices – a breath prayer at your desk, a pause before speaking, a moment of gratitude before bed – are seeds. In the hands of God, seeds never stay small. They carry the power of resurrection. A seed looks ordinary, almost insignificant, yet hidden within it is the mystery of life waiting to unfold. When you plant a seed, you can't see its roots stretching down into the soil, yet they are. You can't see the first shoot pressing upward, and yet it's on its way. In the same way, every small Christ-centered habit carries more weight than you realize in the moment. God takes what feels small, hidden, or ordinary and brings life out of it.

Trust that small, consistent steps bear fruit. Walking with Jesus rarely looks like heroic sprints or dramatic overnight change. More often, it looks like steady faithfulness. One step, then another, and then another. The simple act of showing up with Jesus each day, in small and ordinary ways, creates the space where the Holy Spirit does the deeper work.

Think of clay on a potter's wheel. One press of the hand barely changes its shape. Yet the gentle, repeated touch of the potter transforms a lump of clay into something beautiful and useful. Each prayer, each pause, each choice for compassion is like another press of the Potter's hand. Over time, your life takes on the form God has always envisioned.

One more thing (at least for now). I'd love for you to keep walking this journey with me and others who are seeking to breathe more deeply in Christ. In the *Epilogue,* I'll share how you can be part of the *Breathing in Christ* community where we practice these rhythms together, share encouragement, and keep choosing life with Jesus in the middle of our everyday breaths.

I want to leave you with Jesus' own words and a prayer, the heartbeat behind everything we've explored together: *I am the Vine; you are the branches. Those who abide in me and I in them bear much fruit, because apart from me you can do nothing.*

This is the invitation of Jesus: to abide, to breathe in His life with every breath of your own. Every value you've uncovered, every intention you've named, every habit you've begun, they are all ways of staying rooted in the Vine. Abiding is less about effort and more about presence. As you remain in Christ, fruit will come.

Each practice is a seed. You plant it with your *yes.* The Holy Spirit waters it with grace. Christ Himself gives it breath and life. Sometimes growth will be slow and steady. Other times, it may surprise you with sudden blossoms of joy or peace right when you need them most. Either way, the harvest belongs to God. The promise remains: when you abide in the Vine, your life bears fruit: love, joy, peace, patience, kindness, goodness, faithfulness, gentleness, and self-control. This is resurrection life showing up in ordinary days. This is a life of *Breathing in Christ*.

As you close these pages, remember: you do not walk away empty-handed or alone. The Vine is still holding you. The Gardener is still tending you. The Spirit is still breathing life through you, moment by moment, breath by breath. Welcome home.

A Prayer of Sending

Beloved child of God,

Go in peace, Breathing in Christ.

Root yourself again in the Vine with the One who holds you steady, nourishes your soul, and grows life within you.

May the rhythms you've begun continue to unfold with grace and gentleness.

May your intentions take root in the soil of your daily choices, blossoming into small, steady acts of love.

When the world feels loud and hurried, remember: You are free to pause. You are welcome to rest. You are invited to live from your deepest values because in Christ, your worth has always been secure.

Go now, abiding with Jesus, carried by the Spirit's breath, bearing fruit that will last.

You are seen.

You are held.

You are loved.

Amen.

Epilogue

Breathing Together

MY PRAYER IS that, through these pages, you have received an invitation to rediscover what you were made for: a life rooted in Christ, nourished by His love, and sustained by His Spirit. Wherever you began, I pray you now feel less alone and more deeply grounded in Jesus' promise: "Come to me, all you who are weary and burdened, and I will give you rest" (Matthew 11:28). While this book has pages that end, your journey of *Breathing in Christ* is only beginning.

An Invitation to Keep Breathing

The habits and rhythms you've started here are not meant to stay small or confined to the margins of your journal. They are seeds of resurrection. Tiny beginnings that, when nurtured by the Spirit, grow into the fruit of a Christ-shaped life. You've practiced slowing down enough to notice. You've explored what it means to let go of old stories that no longer serve you and to step into your identity as a beloved child of God. You've discovered that change doesn't have to come through striving or self-improvement. Instead, it comes through small, faithful steps that stack into rhythms of grace. You've learned that your ordinary life – conversations around the dinner table, the way you handle interruptions, even the tone of your voice – can become a living testimony of God's love.

This is the heart of *Breathing in Christ:* to remember that you were never asked to carry life alone, or to manufacture fruit through sheer effort. Jesus, the true Vine, is already holding you. The Spirit is already breathing life through you. God is already tending your growth with care. Your part is simply to stay connected, to keep breathing, and to trust that resurrection power is at work even when you cannot see it. Each breath, each prayer, each small choice to align with Christ is another step into the abundant life you were made for. You began these pages longing for rest. May you carry forward with a deeper rhythm of renewal, awake to Christ's presence in the most ordinary moments of your days.

You don't have to tend those seeds alone. I would love for you to join me in the *Breathing in Christ* community, a digital gathering space where faith and rhythm come together. At *Breathing in Christ*, we believe that living in God's rhythm is more than possible, it's promised. This community is a movement toward Jesus. It's where we remind one another that grace is the air we breathe, that we don't have to hustle for worthiness, and that the Spirit is already at work in the ordinary moments of our lives. We breathe together. We pause to notice God's presence in the everyday. We laugh together, we sometimes cry together, and we keep showing up because transformation doesn't happen overnight. It happens in the small, repeated choices to abide.

If you're longing for encouragement, companionship, and practices that help you live what you've learned in these pages, I invite you to take the next step. Explore the resources, reflections, and offerings at www.breathinginchrist.com. If you're ready to walk this journey with others, you can learn more about joining the membership community here: breathinginchrist.com/collections/memberships. The beauty of community is that we weren't meant to walk alone. Just as the vine grows strongest when its branches grow together, we grow best when we breathe together rooted in Christ, reaching toward the light, bearing fruit for the sake of the world.

So, come breathe with us.

A Word of Gratitude

This book would never have made its way into your hands without the family, friends, and mentors who carried me through seasons of doubt, delay, and discovery. There were days (okay – *months*) when the words wouldn't come, when the vision felt too large, or when I wondered if finishing was even possible. To those who reminded me to breathe when I forgot, to those who listened without judgment, to those who believed in this message before I had the courage to speak it out loud, *thank you*. To my mentors who kept pointing me back to Christ, to the friends who checked in, to my family who gave me the gift of time and space, I am forever grateful. Again and again, the people closest to me offered love, prayer, and patience and, on the days I needed it most, a little "holy pestering" to keep me going. Thank you for your encouragement to live the truths I was writing. Thank you for not giving up on me, even when I was tempted to give up on myself. There are too many to name here. I trust you know who you are. This book is as much the fruit of your love and prayers as it is of my pen and keyboard.

Acknowledgements

NO BOOK IS written alone. This one certainly was not.

Personal Support

My husband Jason and our daughter Gina have been there from the very beginning, encouraging me to keep showing up to write, especially on the days when the words were hard to find.

I am deeply grateful for the family and friends who supported me emotionally throughout this journey. My parents, Sharon and Bill, Lisa, my mother-in-law who patiently offered line-by-line editing, and my sister and brother-in-law, Angela and Chris, all carried this manuscript with encouragement and love. I am also grateful for authentic friends who showed up with support along the way - Ashley, Beth, Katie, Nicole, and Matt, just to name a few.

Writing and Creative Support

Several people offered thoughtful feedback and honest insight as this book took shape. Bill and Melissa generously read early drafts and offered the kind of clarity and honesty every writer needs.

Spiritual Influences

This book has also been nurtured by a circle of spiritual companions who have prayed for this work and helped shape the ideas within it. I am especially grateful for Barb, Beth, Michelle, Patty, and the many others who have listened, reflected, and helped workshop these concepts over the years.

I am also thankful for mentors who have influenced my life and ministry in countless ways including Audrey, Elaine, Gary, Jean, Jim, Mike, Richard, Robyn and Tom.

Professional and Ministry Context

I am deeply grateful to Zion Lutheran Church in Hummelstown, my first calling congregation, where I grew in more ways than I can name. I also give thanks for my years serving on two bishops' staffs, where leaders entrusted me with developing ministry around spiritual wellness and the renewal of leaders and congregations.

I am especially thankful to Dr. Frank Munoz, whose professional medical guidance supported my own health in ways that made this book possible.

My gratitude also extends to the many wellness practitioners who helped open my eyes to the wisdom of creation and the ways the body, spirit, and the natural world participate in God's healing work.

Publishing Support

I am deeply grateful to Bill Huff, who first introduced me to the world of publishing and recognized the need for this book in our world.

Thank you to Pat, Cheryl, and the entire book production team at the Charles Bruce Foundation, whose dedication, skill, and care brought these pages to life.

Those Who Inspired This Book

This book was shaped by the countless leaders and individuals I have walked alongside over the years—people who were exhausted, searching, and longing for the living water Jesus offers. Thank you for trusting me with your stories, your struggles, and your hopes. Your courage to name the deeper longings of the heart has shaped these pages more than you know.

I also want to acknowledge the thousands of artisans who create blankets for the Homeless Memorial Blanket Initiative. Your compassion and dedication are a powerful witness of love and remembrance. This book exists, in part, to support your work.

Faith

In all things, I give thanks to the Holy Trinity—God, Jesus Christ, and the Holy Spirit—whose grace and guidance undoubtedly inspired and sustained this work.

To the Reader

And finally, to you, the reader. May these pages help you experience Jesus in an exhausting world as you discover a life of *Breathing in Christ.*

Bibliography

American Psychological Association. Stress in America™ 2023: A Nation Recovering from Collective Trauma. Washington, DC: American Psychological Association, 2023.

Bowen, Murray. Family Therapy in Clinical Practice. New York: Jason Aronson, 1978.

Brown, Brené. The Gifts of Imperfection. Center City, MN: Hazelden Publishing, 2010.

Clear, James. Atomic Habits: An Easy Proven Way to Build Good Habits & Break Bad Ones. New York: Avery, 2018.

Foster, Richard J. Celebration of Discipline: The Path to Spiritual Growth. New York: HarperOne, 2018.

Hansen, Gary Neal. Kneeling with Giants: Learning to Pray with History's Best Teachers. Downers Grove, IL: IVP Books, 2012.

Jha, Amishi P. Peak Mind: Find Your Focus, Own Your Attention, Invest 12 Minutes a Day. HarperOne, 2021.

McBride, Hillary L. The Wisdom of Your Body: Finding Healing, Wholeness, and Connection Through Embodied Living. Brazos Press, 2021.

National Institutes of Health. "Circadian Rhythms." National Institute of General Medical Sciences. Last modified 2025. https://www.nigms.nih.gov/education/fact-sheets/Pages/circadian-rhythms.aspx

O'Donnell, Kate. Everyday Ayurveda: Daily Habits That Can Change Your Life in a Day. Boston: Shambhala Publications, 2015.

Peterson, Eugene H. The Message: The Bible in Contemporary Language. Colorado Springs, CO: NavPress, 2002.

Sandeman, Stuart. Breathe In, Breathe Out: How the Power of Breath Can Unlock Your Potential. Aster, 2023.

Smith, James K. A. You Are What You Love: The Spiritual Power of Habit. Grand Rapids, MI: Brazos Press, 2016.

Stillman, Cate. Body Thrive: Uplevel Your Body and Your Life with 10 Habits from Ayurveda and Yoga. New York: Wise Ink Creative Publishing, 2015.

Willard, Dallas. Renovation of the Heart: Putting on the Character of Christ. Colorado Springs, CO: NavPress, 2002.

Van der Kolk, Bessel. The Body Keeps the Score: Brain, Mind, and Body in the Healing of Trauma. New York: Viking, 2014.

About Marsha

MARSHA ROSCOE IS an ordained minister, spiritual director, and founder of Breathing in Christ, a ministry devoted to helping people experience Jesus in this exhausting world through Christ-centered rhythms of grace. With more than two decades of ministry experience—including fifteen years serving a congregation and over a decade serving leaders and communities on a bishop's staff—Marsha has accompanied countless individuals navigating seasons of transition, spiritual exhaustion, and a longing to rediscover the life-giving presence of Jesus.

Her work is rooted in a simple but powerful conviction: transformation begins when we slow down, listen deeply for Jesus, and live in rhythm with the life of Christ already breathing within us.

Through teaching, retreats, coaching, and writing, Marsha helps individuals and leadership teams rediscover their identity in Christ, cultivate life-giving rhythms, and learn to breathe again in the presence of God.

Marsha lives in Pennsylvania with her husband, Jason, and their daughter, Gina.